WORLD IN FOCUS

FOCUS ON
Pakistan

SALLY MORGAN

WORLD ALMANAC® LIBRARY

Please visit our web site at: www.garethstevens.com
For a free color catalog describing World Almanac® Library's list of high-quality books
and multimedia programs, call 1-800-848-2928 (USA) or 1-800-387-3178 (Canada).

Library of Congress Cataloging-in-Publication Data available upon request from publisher.

ISBN 978-0-8368-6752-7 (lib. bdg.)
ISBN 978-0-8368-6759-6 (softcover)

This North American edition first published in 2008 by
World Almanac® Library
A Weekly Reader Corporation imprint
200 First Stamford Place
Stamford, CT 06912 USA

Commissioning editor: Nicola Edwards
Editor: Nicola Barber
Inside design: Chris Halls, www.mindseyedesign.co.uk
Cover design: Hodder Wayland
Series concept and project management by EASI-Educational Resourcing
(info@easi-er.co.uk)
Statistical research: Anna Bowden
Maps and graphs: Martin Darlison, Encompass Graphics

World Almanac® Library editor: Alan Wachtel
World Almanac® Library cover design: Scott Krall

Picture acknowledgments. The author and publisher would like to thank the following for allowing their pictures to be reproduced
in this publication:
CORBIS *title page*, 10 (Olivier Matthys/epa), 4, 14 (Galen Rowell), 5 (Lynsey Addario), 6 (Ali Imam/Reuters), 8 (Diego Lezama Orezzoli),
9 (Burstein Collection), 11, 12, 13 (Bettmann), 15, 18, 19 (Ed Kashi), 16, 42 (Mohsin Raza/Reuters), 17 (Amiruddim Mughal/Reuters),
20 (Jonathan Blair), 21, 33, 41, 47 (Akhtar Soomro/epa), 22, 35, 37 (Reuters), 23 (HO/Reuters), 24, 44 (Arshad Arbab/epa), 25, 34, 46, 58
(Mian Khursheed/Reuters), 26, 27 (Rizwan Saeed/Reuters), 28 (Christine Osborne), 29, 39, 55, 57 (Jonathan Blair), 30
(Asim Tanveer/Reuters), 31 (Rahat Dar/epa), 32 (Mimi Mollica), 36, 49 (Zahid Hussein/Reuters), 38 (Athar Hussain/X01601/Reuters),
40 (David Cumming/Eye Ubiquitous), 43 (epa), 45 (Tom Pietrasik), 48, 56 (Maher Attar/MGA Production), 50 (Munish Sharma/Reuters),
51 (Matthieu Paley), 52 (Olivier Matthys/epa), 53 (Paul Almasy), 54 (Shabbir Hussain Imam/epa), 59 (Shawn Thew/epa).

The directional arrow portrayed on the map on page 7 provides only an approximation of north.
The data used to produce the graphics and data panels in this title were the latest available at the time of production.

Printed in China

1 2 3 4 5 6 7 8 9 10 09 08 07

CONTENTS

1 Pakistan – An Overview   4

2 History   8

3 Landscape and Climate   14

4 Population and Settlements   18

5 Government and Politics   22

6 Energy and Resources   26

7 Economy and Income   30

8 Global Connections   34

9 Transportation and Communications   38

10 Education and Health   42

11 Culture and Religion   46

12 Leisure and Tourism   50

13 Environment and Conservation   54

14 Future Challenges   58

Time Line   60

Glossary   61

Further Information   62

Index   63

About the Author   64

Cover: The Badshahi Mosque, in Lahore, is the largest mosque in Pakistan.

Title page: The Badshahi Mosque in Lahore was completed in 1674. It is the largest mosque in Pakistan.

CHAPTER 1

Pakistan – An Overview

Pakistan is the seventh largest country in Asia and occupies a position of great strategic importance. It lies between the Himalaya Mountains and the Arabian Sea and is bordered by Iran to the west, Afghanistan to the northwest, China to the northeast, and India to the east.

The Indus River runs though the center of Pakistan. In about 4000 B.C., people settled in its valley and developed one of the earliest civilizations in the world. The people of the Indus Valley civilization farmed the rich soils of the river plains and used the river as a trade route to the sea. Since then, the plains of the Indus have been fought over and conquered by many different peoples, including Arabs, Mughals, and the British.

Each of these conquering peoples has left their own distinctive mark on the culture of the region. Today, the population of Pakistan is made up of many different groups, each of which has its own culture and language.

YEARS OF STRUGGLE

Beginning in the mid-19th century, the region was part of British India. The modern country of Pakistan was created in 1947 when British India was divided into two separate countries—India and Pakistan. Pakistan was originally made up of two parts. One part was West Pakistan, which extended from the Himalayas along the Indus Valley to the coast. The other, East Pakistan, was a completely separate area between India and Myanmar (Burma). The name "Pakistan" was created using letters taken

▶ Two men cross a wooden bridge over the Indus River in Baltistan, in the Northern Areas of Pakistan. The Indus flows from the mountains southward to the coast near Karachi.

▲ A truck carrying passengers in Karachi. All forms of transportation are seen in Pakistan's cities.

from the names of the different states of the country, namely Punjab, Afghania (North West Frontier Province), Kashmir, Sind, and Baluchistan. The letter *i* was added later to make the name easier to pronounce. In Urdu, the national language of the country, the words *pak* and *stan* mean "pure" and "country."

The years since independence have been eventful, with continual political struggles. Democratically elected governments have been ousted by the military; politicians have been accused of corruption; and there have been assassination attempts on a president. In 1971, East Pakistan broke away to form Bangladesh. Throughout the country's history, some groups have demanded greater representation. Today, some of these groups want independence.

There have been wars, too. Within about a year of its independence, Pakistan was at war with its close neighbor, India, over the mountainous region of Kashmir. Ever since then, Kashmir has been partly occupied by both countries and there have been numerous border disputes, the most serious during the 1990s. In spite of years of talks, the problem has still not been resolved.

Pakistan has had close links with Afghanistan for hundreds of years and, not surprisingly, it has been caught up in the struggles taking place in that country. One problem it has had to cope with is the millions of refugees that have fled across the border to the safety of Pakistan.

GLOBAL SIGNIFICANCE

Pakistan is overwhelmingly Muslim and only a small percentage of people follow other religions, such as Christianity or Hinduism. Pakistan has the second largest Muslim population in the world (after Indonesia), and the country has an important voice in the Islamic world.

For a long time the world powers were not really interested in Pakistan as it was a poor, agricultural nation. But that has changed. Modern-day Pakistan has a booming economy and it occupies an important strategic position between the Middle East and India. Pakistan now has the attention of China and the United States, both countries that are trying to increase their influence in South Asia.

PROBLEMS AHEAD

With nearly 166 million people living in an area slightly less than double the size of California, Pakistan is not without its problems. Birth and death rates are high, and nearly 40 percent of the population is under the age of 15. Many millions of its people live in poverty. The towns

and cities are getting larger, but there is little in the way of urban planning. Streets are congested with traffic, and water supplies and sewage systems are often inadequate. Industrial development is taking place at a fast rate, but there are few environmental controls. As a result, there is widespread disease and pollution.

Physical Geography

- Land area: 300,586 sq miles/778,720 sq km
- Water area: 9,735 sq miles/25,220 sq km
- Total area: 310,321 sq miles/803,940 sq km
- World rank (by area): 35
- Land boundaries: 4,209 miles/6,774 km
- Border countries: Afghanistan, China, India, Iran
- Coastline: 650 miles/1,046 km
- Highest point: K2 (28,253 ft/8,611 m)
- Lowest point: Indian Ocean (0 ft/0 m)

Source: CIA World Factbook

► Muslims pray at Friday prayers in Peshawar. Islam plays an important role in the daily lives of most of the people in Pakistan.

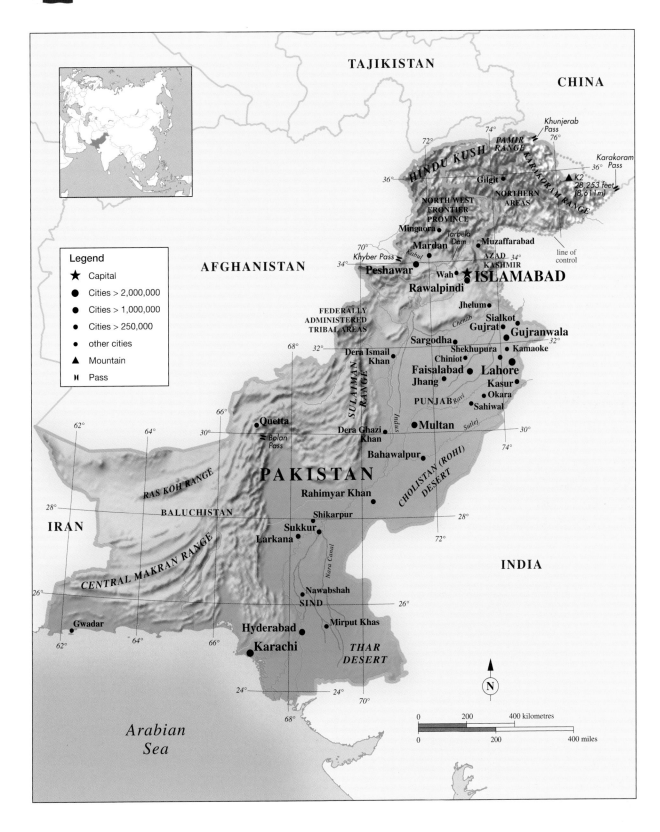

Legend
★ Capital
● Cities > 2,000,000
● Cities > 1,000,000
● Cities > 250,000
• other cities
▲ Mountain
И Pass

TAJIKISTAN

CHINA

Khunjerab
Pass
76°
72°
74°
PAMIR
RANGE
Karakoram
Pass
HINDU KUSH
36°
36°
36°
▲ K2
28,253 feet
(8,611m)
Gilgit
NORTHERN
AREAS
KARAKORAM RANGE
36°
NORTH WEST
FRONTIER
PROVINCE
line of
control
Mingaora
Tarbela
Dam
Muzaffarabad
70°
Mardan
AZAD   34°
KASHMIR
AFGHANISTAN
Khyber Pass И
34°
Kabul
Peshawar
Wah ★ ISLAMABAD
Rawalpindi
Jhelum
FEDERALLY
ADMINISTERED
TRIBAL AREAS
Chenab
Sialkot
Gujrat Gujranwala
Sargodha
Shekhupura   Kamaoke   32°
68°
32°
Dera Ismail
Khan
Chiniot
Faisalabad   Lahore
Jhang
Kasur
Okara
PUNJAB Ravi
Sahiwal
66°
SULAIMAN RANGE
62°
64°
30°
Quetta
Bolan
Pass
Dera Ghazi
Khan
Multan
Sutlej
30°
Indus
74°
Bahawalpur
PAKISTAN
CHOLISTAN (ROHI)
DESERT
28°
RAS KOH RANGE
Rahimyar Khan
72°
BALUCHISTAN
Shikarpur
28°
IRAN
Sukkur
Larkana
INDIA
CENTRAL MAKRAN RANGE
Nara Canal
26°
Nawabshah
SIND
26°
Gwadar
62°
64°
66°
Hyderabad
Mirput Khas
Karachi
THAR
DESERT
24°
24°
70°
68°

Arabian
Sea

N

0   200   400 kilometres
0   200   400 miles

CHAPTER 2

History

As a country, Pakistan came into existence in 1947, but the history of the region that makes up modern-day Pakistan dates back thousands of years, and it includes numerous invasions, military overthrows, and times of political instability.

EARLY HISTORY

The Indus Valley has played an important role in the history of the region. It extends from the Himalayas, in the region's north, to the coast, and it was the site of two of the earliest settlements, Harappa and Moenjodaro, founded between 4000 and 2000 B.C. The first settlers were farmers, attracted by the rich soils that had been built up by the river. Soon, more people moved into the area and settlements formed along the river. Over time, the settlements grew into large, well-planned cities with paved main streets, watchtowers, houses, and meeting halls. This civilization extended from the valley, toward what is now Iran, and into northwest India. The cities traded by sea with Egypt and the Middle East. The Indus Valley civilization came to a sudden end in about 1700 B.C., possibly as a result of devastating floods or a change in the course of the Indus River after an earthquake.

In about 1700 B.C., people from central Asia known as Aryans moved into the Indus Valley looking for grazing land for their herds of cattle. They followed a religion in which they prayed to a mother goddess, which is believed to be the foundation for Hinduism. By 900 B.C., the Aryans had spread across northern India.

GREAT CONQUERORS

The Macedonian general Alexander the Great (356–323 B.C.) was a great conqueror who led his army across the Middle East and Asia, creating a huge empire. In 327 B.C., he entered the Indus Valley where he defeated the army of King Porus, who ruled the region. King Porus used 200 war elephants in the battle. The elephants so terrified Alexander's exhausted troops that, in

► The ruins of the city of Moenjodaro are a UNESCO World Heritage site. The excavated ruins reveal the layout of the sprawling site, with its network of narrow streets.

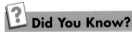

spite of their victory, they mutinied and refused to go any further. By this time, Alexander's empire stretched from Central Europe, south to Egypt, and east to the Punjab. These regions were linked together by a network of trade routes. After Alexander's death, his empire was torn apart by power struggles.

In the Indus Valley, power passed to Chandragupta Maurya in 322 B.C., when he overthrew the royal family of Magadha that had ruled an Indian kingdom to the east since 700 B.C. Chandragupta founded the Mauryan Empire. In 272 B.C., the Mauryan emperor Ashoka came to power. Ashoka was an astute warrior and expanded his empire in a series of campaigns. But after witnessing the carnage that resulted from the last of his conquests, he converted to the new religion of Buddhism and changed his ways. Ashoka helped the spread of Buddhism through South Asia by following Buddhist teachings and by building Buddhist monasteries and *stupas* (memorial buildings).

MANY INVASIONS

During the next few hundred years, the region experienced many invasions, mostly by armies from Europe and Central Asia. Towns and cities were frequently ransacked and people

? Did You Know?

Some of the earliest relics of Stone Age humans, which date back at least 50,000 years, have been found in the Soan Valley, near Rawalpindi in northern Pakistan. The inhabitants of this mainly agricultural region learned to tame and keep animals and cultivate crops about 9,000 years ago. Farming villages dating from 6000 B.C. have been excavated in Baluchistan, the North West Frontier Province, and Punjab.

▲ This sculpture of the Buddha's head dates from the second or third century A.D. and comes from northern Pakistan.

killed. The conquerors brought with them their own languages, cultures, and religions. The invading armies included the Greeks in 195 B.C., the Scythians from Central Asia in 75 B.C., and the powerful Parthians from east of the Caspian Sea in 50 B.C. In A.D. 120, the Parthians were themselves defeated by the Kushans, a people from China. The Kushans established an empire that covered present-day Afghanistan, Pakistan, and northwest India. Under their rule, trade flourished, in particular with the Romans. In the fifth century A.D., White Huns, who were horse-riding nomads from Central Asia, invaded from the north. They, in turn, were defeated by the Sassanians from Persia and by Turks from the eastern Mediterranean. Finally, the region was divided into small kingdoms, each with a Hindu ruler.

UNDER MUSLIM RULE

During the seventh century, Arab armies marched across the Middle East into Persia (now Iran), Afghanistan, and India. The Arabs followed the new religion of Islam, which had started in the Arabian peninsula in the 600s. By 724, the Indus Valley was under the control of a Muslim Arab governor. For about 300 years, the region was divided into two parts. The northern region of Punjab remained under Hindu control, while the south (Multan, Sind, and Baluchistan) was under Muslim rule. Later, the ruler of the state of Ghazni (in present-day Afghanistan), Mahmud Ghaznavi, invaded the Hindu territories of the Punjab and Kashmir and then took control of Baluchistan, creating a state which ruled this region until 1187.

THE SULTANATE PERIOD

The armies of Muhammad of Ghor, invading from Afghanistan, ended the rule of the Ghaznavid Empire. Muhammad's successors established the Delhi Sultanate (1206–1526), under which the region was divided up into states, and each state was headed by a sultan (a Muslim head of state). The sultan was responsible for protecting the state, protecting Islam, enforcing laws, and collecting taxes.

THE MUGHAL EMPIRE

In 1526, the Mughal Empire was founded when the last of the sultans was defeated by Babur, a Muslim ruler from Central Asia whose ancestors included the Mongol emperors Genghis Khan and Timur. Babur conquered the Punjab and much of northern India. The expansion of the Mughal Empire continued under his successors, notably Akbar (who ruled 1556–1605). By 1707, the Mughal Empire stretched across Afghanistan, Punjab, Sind, and Baluchistan, as well as much of India. Under Mughal rule, architecture flourished and some stunning buildings were constructed, including many in Lahore. Starting at the beginning of the 18th century, however, the power of the Mughal rulers began to diminish.

BRITISH RULE

Around 1600, the Britain established a trading partnership with the Mughals. Over the years, the level of trade increased greatly and Britain gradually became involved in the politics of the region. As the Mughals started to lose power, the region became unstable. Britain took advantage of this instability and gradually took control of large areas. In 1857, the War of

▼ The Badshahi Mosque in Lahore, which was completed in 1674, was built by the Mughals. This beautiful mosque is still the largest in Pakistan.

Independence broke out when there was an uprising by both Indian soldiers and local people against Britain. It ended in 1858, when Britain captured and killed the local rulers who they believed were behind the uprising, but not before many thousands of people were killed, including women and children. After these events, Britain claimed sovereignty over much of what is now India and Pakistan and then was known as British India.

HINDUS AND MUSLIMS

Although British India was under Britain's rule, Indians were given limited roles in central and provincial governments beginning in 1909. Many Indian Muslims wanted to play a part in government and still retain their religious identity. The Indian National Congress, founded in 1885, was dominated by Hindus,

so, in 1907, the All-India Muslim League was established. Initially, the main aim of the League was to cooperate with the Hindus to gain independence for India from British rule. However, religious and cultural differences—and the fact that Hindus far outnumbered Muslims—led many Muslims to believe that it would be impossible to have equality with Hindus in India. So the Muslims started to campaign for a new Muslim state that would combine North West Frontier Province, Baluchistan, Punjab, and Sind, as well as Bengal (on the east side of India). During the 1940s, Mohammed Ali Jinnah emerged as the leader of the Muslims. He threatened a civil war in India if the British did not give Pakistan its independence. Finally, in 1947, the British government agreed to divide India into separate parts. In a move known as Partition, the British

Focus on: The Problems of Partition

In 1947, when British India was divided into the two independent nations of Pakistan and India, there were millions of Muslims and Hindus living on the "wrong" sides of the new borders. As a result, about 3.5 million Hindus and Sikhs fled

across the border to India, while 5 million Muslims moved to the new Islamic nation of Pakistan. During this mass migration, violence between Hindus and Muslims left more than half a million people dead.

► Indian refugees crowd onto trains at Amritsar, India, in October 1947. During Partition, millions of Muslims and Hindus fled across the new border.

created the secular nation of India and the Muslim nation of Pakistan. Pakistan was made up of East and West Pakistan. Mohammed Ali Jinnah became the country's governor-general. Pakistan's first constitution was published in 1956, when the country officially became the Islamic Republic of Pakistan.

EAST PAKISTAN

The physical separation of about 1,000 miles (1,600 kilometers) between East and West Pakistan—along with differences in language, culture, and wealth between the two regions—caused major political, economic, and social conflicts within the country. In elections in 1970, the Awami League won nearly all of the seats in East Pakistan, giving it a majority in Pakistan's government in spite of having no representatives in West Pakistan. When the West Pakistanis refused to hand over power to Sheikh Mujib, the leader of the Awami League, there was unrest in East Pakistan. Pakistan's army, which was mostly made up of West Pakistanis, moved into East Pakistan to put

down the uprising, and Sheikh Mujib and other Awami League leaders were arrested. In March 1971, East Pakistan declared its independence and war followed. India's army invaded in December 1971 and quickly defeated West Pakistan's forces. As a result, East Pakistan officially became the independent country of Bangladesh on December 16, 1971. "Pakistan" came to mean what had been West Pakistan.

MARTIAL LAW

On several occasions, Pakistan's military has taken power and governed the country. The first time was in 1958 when government corruption had become widespread, after which there were four years of martial law. Political disputes forced the military to take over again in 1969. But after the embarrassing defeat in East Pakistan, the military government stepped down. In 1971, Zulfiqar Ali Bhutto became

▼ People in Dhaka cheer some of the men who helped East Pakistan—now Bangladesh—gain its independence in December 1971.

president. In 1977, Bhutto was overthrown in a coup led by General Zia-ul-Haq, who imposed martial law. General Zia started a program of Islamization that gave Islam a greater role in everyday life in the country. For example, the teaching of Islamic Studies and Arabic became compulsory. Women, who already had fewer rights than men, found that their freedom was greatly limited. In 1988, General Zia was killed in a plane crash. Benazir Bhutto, the daughter of Zulfiqar Ali Bhutto, became the first woman to govern an Islamic country. She finally lost power in 1996 because of charges that her government was corrupt and mismanaged.

General Pervez Musharraf seized power in 1999. Since the terrorist attacks of September 11, 2001 on the United States, Musharraf has been a strong supporter of the United States and the so-called "war on terror." In 2004, Shaukat Aziz became Pakistan's prime minister and declared his goal of providing good government, legal and police systems, and opportunities for the people of Pakistan.

▲ In September 1988, Benazir Bhutto was elected prime minister of Pakistan. At the time, she was one of the most high-profile female leaders in the world.

Focus on: Problems in Kashmir

At the time of Partition, there were disputes over several states, one of which was Kashmir. Kashmir had a Hindu ruler, but the majority of its people were Muslim, and it had more ties with Pakistan than with India, both geographically and economically. While many people in Kashmir hoped for independence from both countries, Kashmir's ruler decided to sign over the state to India. Pakistan refused to accept this decision, and war broke out in 1948. Kashmir has remained partly occupied by the two countries ever since. The part occupied by Pakistan is called Azad (Free) Kashmir. India and Pakistan fought a second war in 1965, and they have had many border disputes. The most serious of these disputes occurred in the late 1990s, when India and Pakistan moved thousands of troops into the region. Prime Minister Nawaz Sharif negotiated with India over Kashmir, but Pakistan's military did not like the terms to which he agreed. The unhappiness of Pakistan's military resulted in the coup led by General Pervez Musharraf in 1999.

CHAPTER 3

Landscape and Climate

Pakistan is a land of contrasts. Mountains dominate its northern regions; its eastern regions feature deserts, including the Thar Desert; and the mighty Indus River flows through the middle of the country.

MOUNTAINOUS NORTH

The northern highlands of Pakistan include parts of the Hindu Kush, Karakoram, Pamir, and Himalayas mountain ranges. These mountain ranges contain 13 of the world's highest peaks, including K2 at 28,253 feet (8,611 meters), which is the second highest mountain in the world, after Mount Everest, and the highest in Pakistan. In the Himalayas, Nanga Parbat rises to 26,661 feet (8,126 m), while at 25,290 feet (7,708 m), Tirich Mir is the highest mountain in the Hindu Kush. More than half of the peaks in Pakistan exceed 14,764 feet (4,500 m), and more than 50 peaks reach above 21,326 feet (6,500 m).

? Did You Know?

Nanga Parbat ("Naked Mountain" in Urdu) in the western Himalayas is nicknamed the "killer mountain" because it claimed as many as 50 lives before it was successfully climbed by an Austrian mountaineer, Hermann Buhl, in 1953.

▼ A group of mountaineers and porters cross the lower slopes of K2, which is located in the Karakoram mountains in Pakistan's far northeast.

◀ Wells are the only source of water in the desert areas of Pakistan. This well lies in the Cholistan (Rohi) Desert in Punjab Province.

These huge mountain ranges create a barrier between Pakistan and India and Central Asia to the north. There are a number of important high routes, called passes, over the mountains. The main pass is the Karakoram Pass (18,291 feet/5,575 m) that links Kashmir to China. The Khunjerab Pass (15,421 feet/4,700 m) is found on the Pakistan to China route. In the northwest, the Khyber Pass (3,517 feet/1,072 m) links Peshawar, in Pakistan, with Jalalabad, in Afghanistan, where it connects to a route leading to Afghanistan's capital, Kabul. The Bolan Pass (5,879 feet/1,792 m) provides an essential internal link between the two provinces of Baluchistan and Sind.

ARID REGIONS

The Thar, or Great Indian, Desert stretches between northwestern India and southeastern Pakistan. In Pakistan, it extends into the eastern part of Sind Province and the southeastern portion of Punjab Province. About 10 percent of the desert is covered by sand dunes, the highest in the south being about 492 feet (150 m) tall. The rest of the desert is mostly stony desert with rocky outcrops and salt pans. A belt of thorny scrub forest lies around the desert. Some of the desert is irrigated so that people can farm and keep cattle and sheep. Located in the southwest of Pakistan, Baluchistan is a sparsely populated and barren region that has rugged mountains, some fertile river valleys, and desert. This region contains valuable mineral reserves.

THE INDUS VALLEY

The Indus River is the lifeline of Pakistan. The river and its tributaries provide water to two-thirds of the country. The Indus rises in Tibet and flows through Kashmir into Pakistan. It then flows south down the entire length of Pakistan, a distance of about 1,802 miles (2,900 km). The river forms a large delta just before it reaches the Arabian Sea. Over centuries, silt dropped by the waters of the river as they flow downstream has formed a large, fertile plain.

▲ Monsoon rains have flooded this street in Lahore, but daily life goes on as usual.

The amount of silt deposited by the river, however, has fallen in recent years due to the building of dams upstream. Eventually, this will reduce the fertility of the soils, and farmers may have to use artificial fertilizers. All of Pakistan's major rivers flow into the Indus, including the Kabul, Jhelum, Chenab, Ravi, and Sutlej.

CLIMATE

The climate varies across Pakistan. Precipitation ranges from about 6 to 7.9 inches (150 to 200 millimeters) per year in coastal areas to 59 inches (1,500 mm) in the mountains. Winter to summer average temperatures range from -4°F to 32°F (-20°C to 0°C) in the north and from about 57°F to 95°F (14°C to 35°C) in the south.

Much of Pakistan, including Punjab Province, lies in the temperate zone where there are three main seasons: cool and mostly dry from October to February; hot and dry between March and June; and wet and hot from July to September. Islamabad, in the Punjab, has temperatures that range from an average of 48.2°F (9°C) in January to an average high of 90.5°F (32.5°C) in June. The spring monsoon usually starts around May or June, and most of the annual rainfall occurs from July to September. The rest of the year has much less rain—about 2 inches (50 mm) per month or less. The monsoon is unreliable, and some years it fails to arrive altogether, while in others it causes torrential floods.

WATER SHORTAGES

Water supply is a major issue in Pakistan because there is not enough rainfall to support the level of farming needed to grow the country's food and cotton crops, especially in the arid regions around the Thar Desert and in parts of Sind and Baluchistan. Because of this lack, Pakistan relies on an extensive irrigation system using river water from the Indus and its tributaries. The flow of water in the Indus, however, is highly erratic. It depends on water from the monsoon rains and meltwater from the mountains. In some years, the flow of water may be as high as about 7.9 billion cubic feet (223 million cubic meters). In other years, it can fall to as little as about 4.1 billion cubic yards (116 million cubic meters) and no water flows down the river into the sea for several months of the year.

? Did You Know?

Punjab means the "land of five waters." It is named after the five rivers that cross the state: the Indus, Jhelum, Chenab, Ravi, and Sutlej.

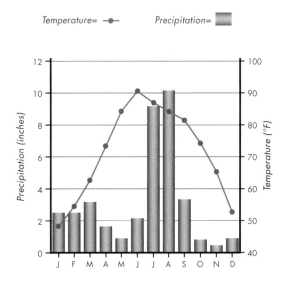

Temperature= ●   Precipitation= ▬

▲ Average monthly climate conditions in Islamabad

Focus on: The 2005 Earthquake

Much of northern Pakistan lies in a zone in which earthquakes are relatively common. In October 2005, the region along the border with Kashmir was struck by an earthquake measuring 7.6 on the Richter scale, the strongest ever to occur in Pakistan. The damage was widespread.

About 80,000 people were killed and up to 100,000 injured in Pakistan and Azad Kashmir. Millions of people were left homeless. In December 2005, it was estimated that repairing and rebuilding in this already poor region would cost more than U.S.$5 billion.

► One month after the 2005 earthquake, a survivor searches the remains of his house in the Neelum Valley, located north of Muzaffarabad in Azad Kashmir. He is looking for useful items such as clothes and cooking utensils.

CHAPTER 4

Population and Settlements

Pakistan is home to nearly 166 million people and has one of the world's fastest growing populations. The current rate of population growth is just over 2 percent, compared to just 0.28 percent in the United Kingdom and 0.92 percent in the United States. At this rate, the population of Pakistan could double by the year 2035. This rapidly increasing population is putting incredible pressure on the country's environment and resources, as well as on its schools and hospitals.

CULTURAL GROUPS

The population of Pakistan is a mixture of many different groups. The main groups include the Punjabis, Sindis, Pathans (also called Pashtuns), Mohajirs, and Baluchis. Within these five main groups are a number of subgroups creating a multilayered cultural mix based on religion, language, and ethnic origin.

The Punjabis are the largest group in Pakistan, making up 48 percent of the population. They live mostly in Punjab Province, and they have their own language, Punjabi. Many Punjabis also both read and speak Urdu, the national language of Pakistan, while a small percentage are also fluent English-speakers (English is the language most often used for official purposes). Punjabis predominate in Pakistan's military and government. Sindis and Pathans are the next largest groups, making up 13 percent and 12.5 percent of the population, respectively. The traditional homeland of the Sindi people is the province of Sind in the southeast of Pakistan. Sindis are mostly rural people with a rich

Population Data

- Population: 165.8 million
- Population 0–14 yrs: 39%
- Population 15–64 yrs: 57%
- Population 65+ yrs: 4%
- Population growth rate: 2.1%
- Population density: 508.7 per sq mile/ 196.4 per sq km
- Urban population: 34%
- Major cities: Karachi 11,819,000
              Lahore 6,373,000
              Faisalabad 2,533,000

Source: United Nations and World Bank

◄ Crowds of people in Lahore walk along Anarkali Street in 2004.

literature and traditions. They prefer to read and write in their own language, Sindi. The Pathans are found in the mountainous north of Pakistan. There are many Pathan subgroups, each one with its own language. Pathans are mostly farmers, traders, or soldiers in Pakistan's army.

MIGRANTS

Mohajirs (meaning "refugees" or "immigrants" in Arabic) are Muslims who migrated from India to the newly formed Pakistan after 1947. They make up about 8 percent of the country's population and are concentrated mostly in the cities of Sind Province, such as Karachi and Hyderabad. They came originally from a variety of different ethnic backgrounds and as a result they have no strong cultural identity, although they all speak Urdu as their native language. So many Mohajirs arrived and settled in Sind Province in the late 1940s that they outnumbered the native Sindi people. The Sindi resented their political and economic influence in the cities, and this caused unrest that increased during the 1960s and continued until very recently. Many Pakistanis still consider the Mohajirs to be outsiders. Many Mohajirs, however, have important roles in government. Pervez Musharraf, for example, comes from a Mohajir family.

▲ Every year, hundreds of tribesmen from Punjab, Baluchistan, and Sind travel with their camels and horses to the Sibi Mela Camel Festival, which is held about 100 miles (160 km) southeast of Quetta.

 Did You Know?

Urdu was chosen to be Pakistan's national language after independence, despite the fact that it was spoken by less than 10 percent of the country's population.

Focus on: Afghan Refugees

The first Afghan refugees started to arrive in Pakistan after the Soviet invasion of Afghanistan in 1979. Over the next 20 years, millions of Afghans fled their country, although many returned after the fall of the Taliban in 2001. In spite of a program of repatriation, 1 million refugees remain in Pakistan's refugee camps. Each year, it costs millions of dollars to provide shelter, food, health care, and other services to the refugees. In 2006, Pakistan's government started another program of repatriation, with the goal of returning 400,000 people to their home country.

Baluchis make up just 4 percent of the population of Pakistan. They are a mostly nomadic people who herd livestock on the arid Baluchistan Plateau. Most Baluchis speak Baluchi, a language that is similar to Persian. They are the least educated and poorest group in Pakistan, and they are not well-represented in government.

EXPANDING CITIES

The urban population of Pakistan is growing rapidly. This growth is both a result of people from rural areas moving to cities for jobs and a consequence of the mass movement of Muslims from India, as many Mohajirs settled in cities in the country's south. By 2005, about 34 percent of Pakistan's population lived in cities. The growth rate of the country's urban population is 4.4 percent, compared with a rate of 2.4 percent for its rural population. About 40 percent of Pakistan's urban population lives in slums— densely populated areas with makeshift housing and few services.

▼ The flat roofs of these houses in Altit, in the Northern Areas of Pakistan, are used for drying fruits in the sun.

THE CAPITAL CITY

After independence and until 1959, Pakistan's capital city was Karachi, in Sind Province in the far south of the country. In 1959, a decision was made to build a new capital city, Islamabad, to reflect the new Pakistan. Islamabad was built in the northwest of the country at the crossroads between Punjab and the North West Frontier Province. This modern city was built beside the ancient city of Rawalpindi, reflecting the country's past and present. Construction started

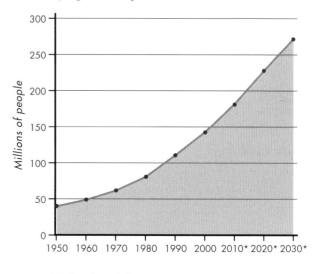

* Projected population

▲ Population growth 1950–2030

Focus on: Land Issues in Karachi

Karachi is a rapidly expanding city, but much of its development is unplanned. A major problem is that too much land is being sold off to meet current demands for developments of new housing and industry with little regard for the future. For example, since 2000, about 988 acres (400 hectares) of land that was originally set aside for facilities such as parks, playgrounds, and sports fields has been built on. The infrastructure of the city cannot cope with such rapid expansion. Corruption is another problem. Some developers illegally change the use of a plot of land from residential to commercial to make the plot more valuable. Also, some government officers sell plots of state-owned land at bargain prices as political favors.

▶ A workman looks out from the shell of a new building overlooking Beach View Park in Karachi in 2005. This building is just one of the many new structures that are being built in the city.

in 1961 and, in 1967, Islamabad officially became the country's capital. Work on the city, however, was not completed until the mid-1970s. The city is divided into eight zones, each with its own particular function, such as government, commerce, or industry.

MAJOR CITIES

Karachi is Pakistan's largest city and its main seaport. It is the capital of Sind Province, and it is a major financial, industrial, and commercial center. The other major city in Sind Province is Hyderabad, which is a manufacturing center with textile and glass factories. It is also a cultural center with museums and mosques.

The Punjab lies in the center of Pakistan and has several large cities, including Lahore,

Pakistan's second largest city and the capital of Punjab Province. Lahore is a cultural and educational center. It is also the main commercial and banking center for the province, and it serves as a distribution center for the heavy industry of the surrounding area. Faisalabad is a center for the textile and fertilizer industries. Multan, in the south of the Punjab, is an ancient city with many Muslim shrines. Rawalpindi, located in northern Punjab, was the temporary capital of Pakistan between 1959 and 1967, while Islamabad was being constructed. It is the headquarters of the Pakistani army and an industrial center. Peshawar is the capital of the North West Frontier Province. Lying near the Khyber Pass, it is a gateway and important trading center between Afghanistan and Southeast Asia.

CHAPTER 5

Government and Politics

Pakistan is a federal republic with Islam as its state religion. There has been considerable political turmoil in Pakistan since independence and the country has been ruled by both democratic and military governments. In the ten-year period following independence there were seven different presidents. This instability led to the military taking over the government.

GOVERNMENT

Pakistan is a federation made up of four self-governing provinces—Baluchistan, Sind, Punjab, and the North West Frontier Province—the Federally Administered Tribal Areas (FATA), and Islamabad Capital Territory, which includes the capital city. The FATA are located along the border with Afghanistan and are mainly inhabited by Pathan tribes. The Pathans are partly independent of Pakistan's central government. Pakistan also has control over Azad Kashmir.

Pakistan's parliament is made up of a National Assembly (lower house) and a Senate (upper house). The 342-member National Assembly has 272 members who are directly elected for five years, while the rest of its members are appointed by the political parties. Sixty of these nonelected seats are reserved for women, and ten are reserved for non-Muslims. The 100 members of the country's Senate are chosen by the four Provincial Assemblies, the FATA, and the Capital Territory. Pakistan's Senate members have a six-year term of office.

The president is Pakistan's head of state, and the prime minister is the chief executive responsible for the day-to-day running of the

▼ The Parliament Buildings in Islamabad. After anti-U.S. violence in 2001, government buildings are guarded by soldiers.

◀ Pakistan's president, Pervez Musharraf (left), and prime minister, Shaukat Aziz (right), shake hands before Musharraf's visit to the United States in 2005.

country. In early 2007, the president was Pervez Musharraf and the prime minister was Shaukat Aziz. Under Pakistan's constitution, the president is elected for a five-year term by the Electoral College of Pakistan, which is made up of the Senate, the National Assembly, and the four Provincial Assemblies. Once elected, the president appoints the leader of the majority party to serve as prime minister. The president is in charge of the country's security, and he or she appoints the head of the army, navy, and air force. He or she also has the power to dissolve the National Assembly and call new elections.

THE CONSTITUTION

Since independence in 1947, Pakistan has had three constitutions, which were adopted in 1956, 1962, and 1973, respectively. The country's constitution was suspended in 1977 after a military coup. In 1985, civilian government was re-established, and the 1973 constitution was restored, although it was altered to increase the powers of the president. In 1997, the democratically elected members of parliament amended the constitution to prevent the president from being able to remove the prime minister and dissolve parliament. Within two years there was another military coup, and Pervez Musharraf seized power. He suspended the constitution, dissolved the democratically elected parliament, and became president. In 2002, Musharraf changed the constitution to strengthen his presidential powers. Only then did he allow the constitution to be restored and parliamentary elections to be held.

 Did You Know?

In the elections of October 2002, 91 women were elected to be members of the National Assembly, the largest percentage of women in parliament in any Muslim-majority country.

LOCAL GOVERNMENT

Each province in Pakistan has its own Provincial Assembly whose members are elected for five-year terms in local elections. The assemblies are responsible for local matters, such as planning and development, legal systems, and providing schools and hospitals. These services are paid for partly by the central government and partly with taxes raised locally. Each assembly elects a chief minister who becomes the executive head of the province. The chief minister chooses a governor.

THE GOVERNMENT AND ISLAM

In some Muslim countries (for example, Saudi Arabia), the laws are based on the Qu'ran, the Muslim holy book. In most Muslim countries, including Pakistan, the laws of the country are not based entirely on the Qu'ran, although the teachings of the Qu'ran make an important contribution to government. A small minority of radical Muslims in Pakistan, however, want Pakistan to become a truly Islamic state. For example, in 2003, the Provincial Assembly of North West Frontier Province, where a number of radical Muslims have been elected, voted to introduce Sharia, or Islamic law. This was the first time this had happened anywhere in Pakistan. Sharia comes from the teachings of the Qu'ran and is a religious code that governs the way people live, from what they wear to when they pray to how they conduct business. Cases are heard by a Sharia court. Within Sharia, certain crimes are punished by specific penalties. Theft, for example, is punished by cutting off a hand. In North West Frontier Province, Sharia now takes precedence over the existing provincial laws, and every Muslim is bound by it.

MAIN POLITICAL ORGANIZATIONS

There are three main political parties in Pakistan, as well as a number of small parties that are campaigning on specific issues. Currently, the largest party in Parliament is the Pakistan Muslim League (Q), or PML-Q. This party is center-to-conservative, and it has its origins in the original Muslim League, which was involved in the foundation of Pakistan. PML-Q was formed in 2001, when the Pakistan Muslim League divided into several parties. PML-Q strongly supports President Pervez

▶ Molana Fazal ur Rehman speaks to supporters during a three-day religious congregation in Peshawar. He is the secretary-general of an Islamic political alliance called Mutahida Majlis-e-Amal.

◀ A Pakistani woman casts her vote during an election at a polling station in Sanjawal, in Punjab Province, in 2004.

Musharraf. Another party, the Pakistan Muslim League (Nawaz), or PML-N, is loyal to Nawaz Sharif. Sharif was twice elected prime minister during the 1990s but escaped the country when Musharraf overthrew his government.

The Pakistan People's Party (PPP) was formed in 1967 with Zulfiqar Ali Bhutto as its chairman. It is a socialist party that wants to improve the standard of living of the poor and to give opportunities to all. There are a number of religious parties that want the Muslim religion to have a greater role in everyday life, with Sharia law replacing the existing legal code. Their share of the vote is small, but they have gained power in areas such as North West Frontier Province.

Focus on: Independence Movements

There are more than 16 million Pathans living in northern Pakistan and Afghanistan. The Pathans are a fiercely independent people who have a long history of resisting invaders, including the British. In 1902, Britain gave the Pathans the region of North West Frontier Province, between the border of British India and Afghanistan. After 1947, a Pathan independence movement called the Redshirts was formed to campaign for an independent Pushtunistan. The independence of Bangladesh in 1971 encouraged the Pathans to demand more control over their land, resulting in thousands of armed Pathans clashing with the Pakistani military. There has been civil unrest in the region ever since.

There is also a movement for independence in Baluchistan. Baluchistan is a poor province and its people have seen little benefit from the region's large gas fields. Only 25 percent of its villages have electricity and only 20 percent have safe drinking water. The outlawed Baluchistan Liberation Army carries out frequent attacks on gas pipelines and electrical pylons, often disrupting the flow of oil, gas, and electricity to the rest of Pakistan.

CHAPTER 6

Energy and Resources

Pakistan's energy consumption has tripled since 1985, and it is continuing to rise, as industry develops and more villages are connected to the electricity grid. The country is not particularly rich in natural resources. Pakistan has oil and gas fields, as well as coal deposits, but its production of these fuels is not sufficient to meet demand, so the country relies on expensive imports.

FOSSIL FUELS

Pakistan is heavily dependent on imported oil. In 2002, imported oil represented 31 percent of the country's energy consumption at a cost of about U.S.$3.1 billion. The most productive of the country's oil fields is at Dhurnal in Punjab Province, but production is now declining. In contrast, Pakistan's natural gas fields are substantial and at the moment they can supply all the country's needs. Most of the country's gas fields, however, are in Baluchistan and pipelines are attacked regularly. The gas is distributed via a network of pipelines and is used for electricity generation and industrial uses. Demand for gas is growing at 6.3 percent per year. By 2010, Pakistan will have to import gas to make up the difference between production and demand.

Pakistan's largest reserves of coal—about 480 tons (435 billion metric tons)—are located in Sind Province, with smaller coal deposits in Punjab and Baluchistan. Pakistan's coal is of

▼ The purification plant at the Sui gas field in Baluchistan in 2006. The average output of this gas field is about 1 billion cubic feet (28 million cubic meters) per day, representing almost 45 percent of the country's total natural gas production.

◀ Local people wait for news outside a coal mine near Quetta after an underground gas explosion in 2004. Fifteen miners died in the explosion.

low grade and low value. Most of the country's coal is used in power stations that generate electricity for its brick-making industry.

MORE ELECTRICITY

In 2004, Pakistan's government published its 25-year Energy Security Plan. The country has ambitious plans to increase its electricity-generating capacity from 19,000 megawatts to 160,000 megawatts by 2030. The only way this can be achieved without importing more oil is by developing renewable energy sources such as hydroelectric power (HEP), wind power, and solar energy.

 Did You Know?

In 2002, less than half of Pakistan's population had access to electricity.

Focus on: Nuclear Power

Nuclear power provides about 2.2 percent of total electricity production in Pakistan. The country has two nuclear power plants, powered by uranium, which is quarried in Pakistan. The first plant, a pressurized water reactor, was built in the 1970s on the coast near Karachi with help from Canadian companies. It has recently been upgraded so it can operate until 2012. Pakistan's second nuclear plant, at Chasma in the Punjab, was built with the help of China. Pakistan is in negotiations with China to build two more nuclear reactors at the two existing sites. Nuclear power plants generate toxic waste that either has to be placed in underground long-term storage or sent for reprocessing. The small amount of toxic waste generated by the country's two nuclear power plants is currently stored.

HEP has the potential to generate up to 50,000 megawatts of electricity, but only about 6,500 megawatts were being generated by 2005. The country's two main hydroelectric dams are the Tarbela Dam, on the Indus, and the Mangla Dam, on the Jhelum River in Azad Kashmir. More HEP programs are planned, including the Basha Dam, which is upstream from the Tarbela Dam. HEP is a sustainable source of power, but it has problems. For example, a dam traps silt in its reservoir rather than letting the silt be deposited in the river valley, gradually reducing the output of the dam. This problem can be addressed by catching the silt before it enters the reservoir and by planting trees on cleared slopes to stop soil from being eroded. Dams also reduce the flow of water down a river which can interfere with irrigation and disrupt the movement of fish.

RENEWABLE ENERGY

Pakistan aims to generate 5 percent of its electricity using renewable energy sources other than HEP by 2030. For example, two new wind farms under construction in Sind Province will generate a total of 700 megawatts by 2010. About 60 percent of Pakistan's villages are not connected to the electricity grid. Because the cost of extending the grid into remote areas is high, small-scale renewable energy programs are more appropriate in these areas. Microwind turbines, for example, are being installed in many places in Sind Province to provide electricity and power for pumping water. Solar power units are being fitted to houses to supply power to lighting, fans, electric sockets, solar water disinfectant units, and solar cookers.

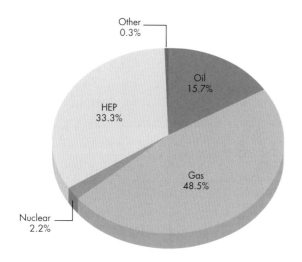

▲ Electricity production by type

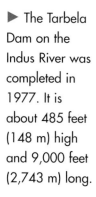

► The Tarbela Dam on the Indus River was completed in 1977. It is about 485 feet (148 m) high and 9,000 feet (2,743 m) long.

WATER RESOURCES

In 2003 and 2004, widespread drought in Sind Province caused the water level in water-bearing rocks (aquifers) to fall by 33 feet (10 m). With a population expected to nearly double by 2035, water supplies are critical to Pakistan's survival. As the country's water demands increase, Pakistan needs to start building reservoirs to store large amounts of water. Agriculture uses about 95 percent of the country's water to irrigate about 36 million acres (14.6 million hectares) of farmland, but the irrigation systems are poorly managed. Up to one-quarter of the irrigated land is waterlogged and this has led to major problems with salinization.

Energy Data

- Energy consumption as % of world total: 0.7%
- Energy consumption by sector (% of total):
  Industry: 26.7%
  Transportation: 17.3%
  Agriculture: 1.4%
  Services: 2.5%
  Residential: 51.6%
  Other: 0.5%
- CO_2 emissions as % of world total: 0.4%
- CO_2 emissions per capita in tons per year: 0.79

Source: World Resources Institute

▲ In the far north of Pakistan, men dig an irrigation channel to carry water from a glacier to newly planted orchards and fields in the valley below.

Focus on: The Indus Waters Treaty

Pakistan depends almost entirely on water from the Indus basin. In 1960, a dispute between Pakistan and India over the use of water from the Indus basin was resolved by the Indus Waters Treaty. Under this treaty, Pakistan receives most of the flow of the Indus, Jhelum, and Chenab Rivers. In 2000, however, India started construction of the Baglihar Dam on the Jhelum, sparking fears of a "water war." In 2005, Pakistan took the issue to the World Bank, which had mediated in the original treaty between Pakistan and India. Pakistan claims that the Baglihar Dam will deprive it of water for agriculture and HEP programs. Pakistan's government also fears that in times of tension, India could use the dam gates to cause a flood or to withhold water. Discussions in 2006 indicated that an agreement between the two countries was likely.

CHAPTER 7

Economy and Income

In 1947, Pakistan's economy was based on agriculture, with virtually no industry and few financial or energy resources. Since then, the country's reliance on agriculture has decreased, and industry and manufacturing have steadily developed. In 2005, Pakistan had the second-fastest growing economy in Asia, beaten only by China.

AGRICULTURE

Despite the shift away from agriculture to industry, farming still employs about 50 percent of Pakistan's working population. In 2004, agriculture contributed 22 percent to Pakistan's GDP . The country's chief crops include cotton, wheat, rice, sugar cane, and tobacco. Pakistan is the world's fourth largest cotton producer, and cotton and textiles make up two-thirds of the country's export earnings. The cotton crop covers about 7.9 million acres (3.2 million hectares), most of which is in Punjab Province.

MANUFACTURING AND TRADE

Pakistan's manufacturing capacity has expanded steadily since independence. In 2004–2005, it accounted for about 18 percent

Focus on: Cotton Production

Between 2002 and 2003, Pakistan produced just under 12 million bales of cotton (each bale weighing 375 pounds [170 kilograms]), an increase from about 9.3 million bales in the 1990s. The yield for 2005–2006 was estimated to be 15 million bales. This was achieved by planting higher-yielding cotton varieties and by improving irrigation and pest control; pests such as the leaf curl virus can destroy cotton. The size of the country's crop is important as it determines the availability and cost of cotton for its textile industry, which influences the value of its exports. In spite of the increases in yield, Pakistan's demand for cotton exceeds its domestic harvest. Because of this demand, Pakistan imports between 1.2 and 1.5 million bales of high-grade cotton, making the country the world's third largest importer of cotton. Most cotton imported to Pakistan comes from the United States.

▲ A worker in a cotton field near Multan. The delicate cotton is picked off the plants by hand.

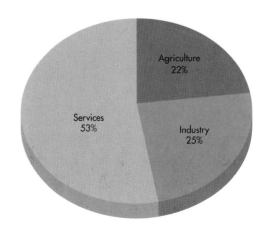
◀ A worker packs boxes with soccer balls for sale during the 2006 World Cup. About 85 percent of the world's soccer balls are manufactured in factories in Sialkot, in Punjab Province.

of the country's GDP. Textiles is Pakistan's largest manufacturing sector, followed by cement, sugar, and rubber. Manufacturing industries employ just under 20 percent of the country's workforce. Its main manufacturing centers include Karachi, Hyderabad, and the region around Lahore.

Pakistan has a number of major trading partners, of which Europe, the United States, and China are among the largest. The country's main imports include wheat, cotton, oil, chemicals, fertilizers, machinery, and transportation equipment, while its exports consist mostly of textile and agricultural products. Pakistan imports a lot of oil, mostly from neighboring Iran. Pakistan has also improved trade with India; a four-year ban on sugar imports was lifted in 2005.

Economic Data

- 🗁 Gross National Income (GNI) in U.S.$: 90,663,000,000
- 🗁 World rank by GNI: 44
- 🗁 GNI per capita in U.S.$: 600
- 🗁 World rank by GNI per capita: 161
- 🗁 Economic growth: 6.4%

Source: World Bank

Agriculture
22%

Services
53%

Industry
25%

▲ Contribution by sector to national income

GROWTH RATES

During the 1980s, Pakistan's economy grew at about 6 percent annually. This high growth rate was created by aid from the United States, money sent back home by Pakistanis working abroad, and bumper crops of cotton and wheat. During the 1990s, Pakistan's economy slowed, partly as a result of poor management and corruption in the higher levels of government. Since 2000, the country's growth rate has risen. In 2005, it reached a record high of more than 8 percent. Since 2005, however, inflation in Pakistan has risen to 11 percent. This increase has been caused by higher oil prices and by food producers limiting the supply of foodstuffs in order to push prices up. In spite of the country's record economic growth, Pakistan's rate of unemployment was still 6.6 percent in 2005, and poverty is widespread in the country.

WOMEN AT WORK

Traditionally in Pakistan, it is considered improper for a woman to work. This attitude is changing in some parts of the country, particularly in its cities. Usually, only the poorest women work outside the home, often as midwives, cleaners, or nannies. Some women work from home making goods that they sell to

Focus on: Pakistanis Abroad

During the 1970s, unemployment was high in Pakistan, so the government encouraged workers to travel abroad for work, especially to the Middle East. Today more than 2 million Pakistanis—about 2 percent of the adult male workforce—live outside Pakistan, three-quarters of them in the Gulf States. Most send money to their families, and, for this reason, they are Pakistan's second-largest source of foreign exchange (about U.S.$2.5 billion in 2002). Pakistani migrant workers usually stay between three and six years in the Middle East and are often then replaced by another family member. Most are unskilled or semiskilled workers under 30 years old, often from the northern provinces.

▶ This Pakistani-born bus driver is working in Britain.

▶ A homeless man sleeps next to a busy road in Karachi in 2005. Extreme poverty is a major problem in Pakistan.

middlemen, often for very little money. Few families admit that their women work for fear of being shamed, and this makes it difficult for poorer women to improve their chances of employment and to be protected against exploitation. Women from richer families tend to be well-educated, and some have held important roles in government.

DEBT AND POVERTY

Although Pakistan is a growing economy, it has relatively small amounts of money to spend on public services. The army is large and expensive to run, the population is increasing rapidly, and the millions of Afghan refugees in the country need both food and shelter. The country also has a huge foreign debt, which stood at about U.S.$34 billion in 2005. These facts mean that more than 80 percent of Pakistan's annual budget is spent on paying back its foreign debt, paying for the army, and for general administration. Less than 20 percent is left for public services such as health and education.

Poverty is a major problem in Pakistan. In 2002, about 35 percent of the population—one out of every three people—lived below the poverty line of U.S.$2 a day, an increase from 26 percent in 1988. These people lack sufficient food and access to basic services, schooling, and health care. Many of the country's poor live in rural areas where they are vulnerable to problems caused by water pollution and soil erosion.

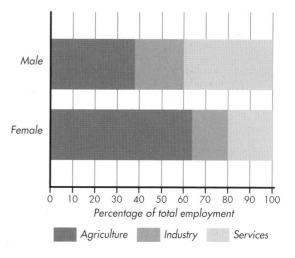

Percentage of total employment

◼ Agriculture   ◼ Industry   ◼ Services

▲ Labor force by sector and gender

CHAPTER 8

Global Connections

Pakistan has a significant voice in the Muslim world and in South Asia, and its control over vital routes through the mountains and access to trade routes through the Arabian Sea make it an important regional power.

INDIA AND PAKISTAN

India and Pakistan have never agreed over the status of Kashmir, and there have been border disputes since independence. During the 1990s, diplomatic talks broke down and thousands of troops were moved into the region. Tension grew in 1998 when, first India and then Pakistan carried out nuclear tests, resulting in economic sanctions being put in place against both countries by the United States, the European Union, and other trading partners. This test marked the first time Pakistan publicly admitted to having nuclear weapons. In fact, Pakistan had been secretly developing nuclear weapons since the 1970s, after India tested its own nuclear device in 1974. In April 1999, when Pakistani soldiers and Kashmiri militants crossed into Indian territory, the Indian army attacked, resulting in armed hostilities known as the Kargil Conflict. After a great deal of international diplomacy, Pakistan agreed to withdraw in June 1999. But military build-up in the area continued, and by 2002, the two countries had an estimated 1 million troops along the border. Outright war over Kashmir, however, was averted by ongoing international diplomacy, and in 2004, India and Pakistan agreed to a ceasefire. Since then relations between the two countries have improved, allowing, for example, cross-border bus services to resume in 2005.

▼ Pakistani soldiers stand at a checkpoint along the Line of Control that divides Pakistani-controlled Kashmir from Indian-controlled Kashmir.

FRIENDS WITH CHINA

After the war with India in 1965, Pakistan developed strong ties with China, and the relationship between the two countries has grown stronger over the years. Today, China is one of Pakistan's major trading partners, and it has played a critical role in financing much of Pakistan's industrial development, in particular the building of nuclear reactors and the modernization of the railway network. China gains access to trade routes and influence in the region through this relationship.

AFGHANISTAN

Pathans live in both Afghanistan and Pakistan, so historically there have been close links between the two countries. When the Soviet Union invaded Afghanistan in 1979, Pakistan's

▶ Refugees wait to enter Pakistan from Afghanistan at a border crossing in Baluchistan in 2001. Since 1979, more than 3 million Afghan refugees have fled to Pakistan.

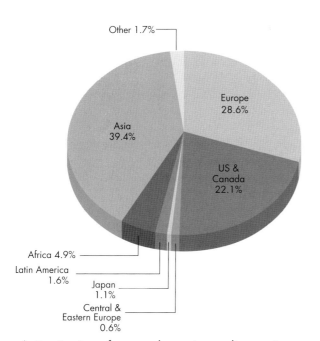

Other 1.7%
Europe 28.6%
Asia 39.4%
US & Canada 22.1%
Africa 4.9%
Latin America 1.6%
Japan 1.1%
Central & Eastern Europe 0.6%

▲ Destination of exports by major trading region

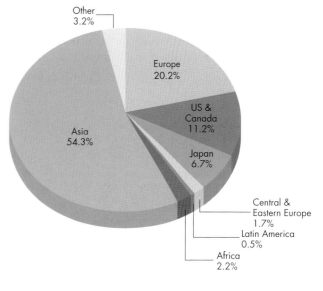

Other 3.2%
Europe 20.2%
US & Canada 11.2%
Asia 54.3%
Japan 6.7%
Central & Eastern Europe 1.7%
Latin America 0.5%
Africa 2.2%

▲ Origin of imports by major trading region

Did You Know?

Between 1979 and 1990, more than 3.3 million Afghan refugees crossed the border into Pakistan.

government played a vital role in supporting anti-Soviet forces and sheltering millions of Afghan refugees. The Soviet army withdrew in 1989, but fighting between rival groups meant that millions of Afghan refugees remained in Pakistan. In 1996, the Taliban, an Islamic fundamentalist group, took control and set up an Islamic government in Afghanistan, which was supported by Pakistan.

FRIEND OF THE UNITED STATES

The United States has played an important role in Pakistan since 1947. During the early 1950s Pakistan was described as the United States's "most allied ally in Asia" by a Pakistani military leader, but this changed during the 1960s when Pakistan went to war with India. During the 1980s, the United States provided Pakistan with military aid to support the anti-Soviet forces in

Afghanistan. In 1998, the United States imposed economic sanctions on both Pakistan and India after they carried out nuclear tests.

The relationship between Pakistan and the United States improved once again after the terrorist attacks in the United States in September 2001. The terrorists were members of al-Qaeda, a group based in Afghanistan, led by Osama bin Laden, and supported by the Taliban. Following the attacks, U.S. president George W. Bush announced a "war on terrorism," and his first action was to invade Afghanistan to remove the Taliban regime and try to find bin Laden. President Musharraf was put under considerable international pressure to align his government with the United States, despite objections from within his own country. Pakistan withdrew its diplomats from Afghanistan, officially closed its borders, and arrested Islamic radicals. During the invasion of Afghanistan, the United States military was permitted to use Pakistan's air space.

◄ This picture shows the scene outside the U.S. consulate in Karachi in March 2006, just after a car bomb exploded. The attack happened two days before the visit of U.S. president George W. Bush to Pakistan.

▶ President Pervez Musharraf listens to UN secretary-general Kofi Annan during a Human Development Forum held in Islamabad in 2002.

REGIONAL ORGANIZATIONS

Pakistan is a member of a number of regional organizations including the Organization of the Islamic Conference (OIC) and the South Asian Association for Regional Cooperation (SAARC). The OIC is an intergovernmental organization that is dedicated to representing the world's Muslims, and it has a permanent delegation at the United Nations. SAARC is a South Asian organization whose members meet regularly to improve regional cooperation, to promote economic development, and to address the social welfare problems of member states. Pakistan is also a member of the Commonwealth of Nations, an organization made up of the former territories of the British Empire. Pakistan left the Commonwealth in 1972 in protest of the Commonwealth's recognition of Bangladesh, but it rejoined the group in 1989.

Focus on: Musharraf's Balancing Act

Musharraf's cooperation with the United States since 2001 has been met with hostility from Islamic fundamentalist groups within Pakistan and disapproval from other Muslim countries. Despite the fact that the United States has provided large sums of financial aid to Pakistan, President Musharraf nevertheless came under pressure from political parties within Pakistan to end the friendship with the United States. In 2002 violent riots and anti-U.S. demonstrations occurred in many cities in Pakistan, and the U.S. journalist Daniel Pearl was kidnapped and murdered by Islamic extremists in Pakistan. In 2003, President Musharraf himself survived two assassination attempts. As a result of these attacks, Musharraf cracked down on the fundamentalists and directed Pakistan's army to hunt for al-Qaeda and Taliban forces along Pakistan's border with Afghanistan. In 2004, U.S. president George W. Bush designated Pakistan as a major non-NATO ally, a status that allows Pakistan to purchase advanced American military technology.

CHAPTER 9

Transportation and Communications

Most of Pakistan's major road and rail routes run from north to south along the valley of the Indus River, with few routes into the mountains. Until 1990, little investment had been made in the transportation network of the country.

ROADS

Much of Pakistan's rural road network is in poor condition with roads consisting of a narrow strip of tarmac with dirt and gravel on either side. The few roads through the mountains are frequently blocked by landslides or washed away by floods. During the 1990s, Pakistan started a huge project to construct a network of major roads to connect its main cities and towns. To help fund this expensive project, the government encouraged private companies to invest in the new roads. For example, the South Korean company Daewoo built the highway between Islamabad and

Transport & Communications Data

- ▭ Total roads: 158,090 miles/254,410 km
- ▭ Total paved roads: 94,854 miles/152,646 km
- ▭ Total unpaved roads: 63,236 miles/101,764 km
- ▭ Total railways: 5,072 miles/8,163 km
- ▭ Major Airports: 91
- ▭ Cars per 1,000 people: 7
- ▭ Cellular phones per 1,000 people: 33
- ▭ Personal computers per 1,000 people: 5
- ▭ Internet users per 1,000 people: 13

Source: World Bank and CIA World Factbook

◀ In 2006, hundreds of auto rickshaw drivers took part in a rally in Karachi to protest government plans to ban their vehicles because of the amount of pollution they produce.

Focus on: The Karakoram Highway

The Karakoram Highway was opened in 1982 after 20 years of construction. It connects Islamabad with Kashgar (also known as Kashi) in China, a distance of 808 miles (1,300 km) through the Karakoram Mountains. Between 500 and 800 Pakistanis and a similar number of Chinese died during its construction. Not only is this road a vital trade link with China, it is also important to the military because it lies close to Kashmir.

▼ Tourists take a drive along the dramatic Karakoram Highway.

Lahore. This road was completed in 1997. Until 2008, when the highway will be handed over to Pakistan's government, Daewoo charges drivers a toll to use the road. Daewoo is responsible for its maintenance.

CONGESTION

The number of vehicles on Pakistan's roads is increasing rapidly. This growth in traffic is causing major congestion problems, because many streets in Pakistan's cities were not designed for large numbers of vehicles.

Emissions from cars and other vehicles are also partly responsible for high levels of air pollution in many of Pakistan's cities. In response to the traffic chaos in Karachi, the first mass transit project in Pakistan is being built in the city. This system is designed to move large numbers of people swiftly around the city, and it should be complete by 2008. Much of its first phase will be a light-rail link built over the existing road system. Plans exist for a second phase, which will involve a subway system, to be built as soon as the first phase is complete.

RAILWAYS

The country's railway network is run by Pakistan Railways, and it carries more than 65 million passengers each year. As well as passenger trains, Pakistan has an extensive freight transportation system that connects the port of Karachi with the country's major cities and industrial centers. The rail network is being modernized. The entire 1,094-mile (1,760-km) track between Peshawar and Karachi has been replaced. New engines, coaches, and track have been purchased from China. The first of the new coaches started running on the Lahore-to-Karachi line in 2002, and it has been named the Karakoram Express.

PORTS

Karachi is the principal port of Pakistan. In 2002, construction started on a new port at Gwadar, near Pakistan's border with Iran, on the west coast of Baluchistan. The goal of building this port is to reduce Pakistan's dependence on Karachi—which is very close to its border with India. The cost is huge, an estimated U.S.$1.16 billion. Because the new port will provide China with vital access to major shipping routes and strengthen China's trade links with the Middle East and Europe, China has provided much of the funding, construction engineers, and technical expertise for the project. In addition, a new highway, also funded by China, is being built between Gwadar and Karachi.

COMMUNICATIONS

Television broadcasting in Pakistan started in 1964. Since then, it has expanded to provide almost complete coverage of the country, even the mountainous regions. Satellite television arrived in Pakistan in the early 1990s, bringing

▼ Railway stations in Pakistan's major cities, such as this one in Karachi, are busy places.

◀ A woman in Karachi walks past a wall of advertisements for cellular phones. Sales of cellular phones are booming in Pakistan, especially among young people.

international broadcasting to nearly all homes. Cable television companies also operate in Pakistan's cities. The country's television channels were run by the state-owned Pakistan Television until 2002, when the government opened up the television market and allowed privately owned channels to broadcast.

Until 2000, few people in Pakistan had a telephone. Landlines were found mostly in urban areas, and very few people in rural areas had access to a phone. Since the arrival of cellular phones in 1990, transmitters have been erected across the country, enabling people in both urban and rural areas to use phones. In 2004, cell phones and cellular service came down in price, and more people could afford them. By 2004, Pakistan had more than 5 million cell phones in use.

Internet use is also increasing in Pakistan. New high-speed fiber-optic connections link cities, allowing Pakistan to compete with other countries in fields such as information technology (IT). By 2006, it is predicted that more than 80 percent of the country's

population will have access to the Internet. Pakistan, however, had only about 2 million Internet users in 2004—one of the lowest numbers of any country in the world.

Did You Know?

It is estimated that by 2007 the number of people in Pakistan owning a cellular phone will exceed the number owning a landline phone. In Pakistan, the cellular phone has become a necessity rather than a luxury.

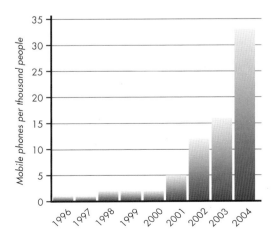

▲ Cellular phone use, 1996–2004

CHAPTER 10

Education and Health

Over the last 30 years, Pakistan's government has spent increasing amounts of money on schools and health care. The country's population has been growing so fast, however, that it cannot keep up with demand.

SCHOOLING

Pakistan has one of the lowest literacy rates in the world. In 1998, the government launched a 12-year program to wipe out illiteracy and provide all children with primary education. In 1998, only 40 percent of adult Pakistanis could read. The country's goal was to double this by 2010. But by 2004, the adult literacy rate had increased to just 49.9 percent.

Primary school education in Pakistan is free but not compulsory. Children attend primary school for five years. About 75 percent of boys complete their primary education but only about 50 percent of girls stay for all five years. Class sizes can be as large as 50 or 60 children, and school facilities are often very basic. Some schools, for example, lack toilets.

Children in Pakistan go to secondary school between the ages of 11 and 18. Secondary education in the country is not free, so only about one quarter of children attend these

Education and Health

- Life expectancy at birth male: 64.1
- Life expectancy at birth female: 65.7
- Infant mortality rate per 1,000: 81
- Under five mortality rate per 1,000: 103
- Physicians per 1,000 people: 0.7
- Health expenditure as % of GDP: 2.4%
- Education expenditure as % of GDP: 2%
- Primary school net enrollment: 56%
- Student-teacher ratio, primary: 46.9
- Adult literacy as % age 15+: 49.9%

Source: United Nations Agencies and World Bank

◀ These Muslim students attend a madrassa in Lahore. Each day madrassa students spend many hours reading and learning about the Qu'ran.

Focus on: Education for Girls

Fewer than 50 percent of girls go to school in Pakistan. Some parents feel it is a waste of time to educate girls, while others cannot afford the cost of secondary schools. Another reason for nonattendance is religion. Many Muslim girls are not allowed to leave home without an escort, so getting to school can be difficult. Also, there may be fears about young girls being seen by men outside the home. Often this problems can be overcome by simply building a wall around a school, so that girls can study in privacy. There has been a government program over about the last 20 years to persuade more parents to send their daughters to school. The literacy rate among women in Pakistan has risen from 21 percent in 1980 to 34 percent in 2004.

▲ A lesson at a school in Meerwala, in Punjab Province. In recent years the number of girls attending school in Pakistan has increased.

schools. These students must study Urdu, English, Pakistani Studies, and Islamic Studies. They take the secondary-school certificate exam at 15 years old, which they must pass if they want to attend higher secondary school until they are 18. At the end of higher secondary school, students take the higher-secondary certificate exam, which is required for study in a university. Many children from richer families are sent to English-speaking schools, followed by university in Europe or North America.

RELIGIOUS SCHOOLS

There are as many as 40,000 private Islamic schools, called madrassas, in Pakistan. They educate between 1 million and 3 million pupils, most of whom are boys between the ages of 8 and 15. Many poor families send their boys to these schools as they offer free education. Most madrassas focus on teaching the Qu'ran, but Pakistan's government is trying to persuade these schools to teach a full range of subjects in return for funding.

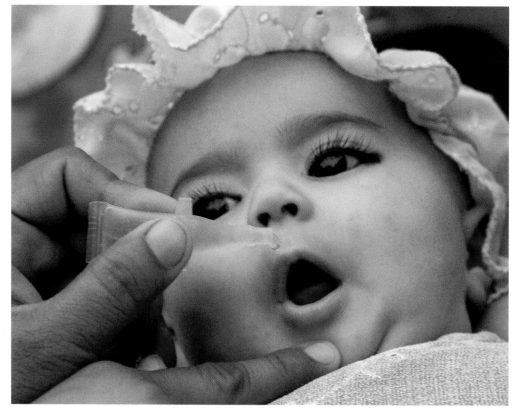

► Pakistan's government has a program to vaccinate all children under the age of five against polio. The polio vaccine is given as drops in the mouth.

HEALTH

The health of the people of Pakistan has improved over the last 30 years. The country's health-care system, however, is struggling to keep up with the growing number of people.

Each year, many children in Pakistan die from preventable diseases such as measles and diarrhea. Over the last ten years, there has been a massive vaccination program in the country, and this is beginning to reduce the number of children dying from infectious diseases such as tetanus, polio, and whooping cough. Although the number of children dying before they reach

 Did You Know?

Each year about 270,000 people in Pakistan catch tuberculosis, a disease of the lungs caused by a bacterium. It can be treated with antibiotics.

five years of age has decreased—down from 130 deaths per 1,000 in 1990 to 103 deaths per 1,000 in 2003—their mortality rate is still higher than that of children in India (87 deaths per 1,000) and Bangladesh (69 deaths per 1,000).

WOMEN'S HEALTH

Women in Pakistan suffer from more health problems than men. Most of their health problems are linked to large family sizes and the frequency with which they give birth. The average family in Pakistan has five to six children, much higher than elsewhere in South Asia. Every year in Pakistan there are about five million births, and as many as 30,000 women die of pregnancy-related complications. The underlying problems that affect women's health include poverty, illiteracy, women's low status in society, inadequate water supplies, and poor sanitation. One way to reduce this death rate is through family planning and the use of contraceptives. Contraceptives, however, need to be used correctly if they are to work. With more women in the country able to read, more women will be able to follow instructions to use contraceptives to prevent unwanted pregnancy.

One government project to help improve women's health is called the Lady Health Worker Program. Many women have problems leaving the house because they need permission from their husbands, and they cannot have male visitors. The Lady Health Worker Program provides female health workers to visit women in their homes. These workers make sure that women are familiar with all issues associated with their health, teach some basic health care, and provide family planning. In 2005, about 43,000 women were serving as Lady Health Workers in their home villages.

POLLUTION AND HEALTH

Many health problems in Pakistan are caused by air and water pollution. Raw sewage is dumped into rivers and the presence of bacteria in the water causes diseases such as dysentery and cholera. Cars with poorly maintained engines and cars that burn poor-quality fuel are the country's main source of air pollution. Up to 6.5 million people in Pakistan are hospitalized each year for illnesses related to air pollution.

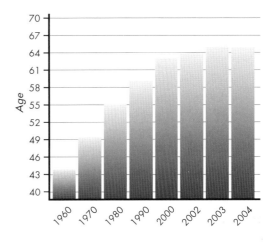

▲ Life expectancy at birth 1960–2004

▼ The Shaukat Khanum Memorial Hospital in Lahore is a world-class cancer hospital. It treats 2,500 new patients each year.

CHAPTER 11

Culture and Religion

Pakistani society is multilingual and multicultural. Traditional Islamic family values are highly respected. Over the last few decades, a middle class has emerged in many of the larger cities for whom education, home ownership, and career prospects are important. In contrast, the people of northwest Pakistan are highly conservative and practice centuries-old customs.

FOOD

Pakistani food is a mix of Middle Eastern and northern Indian traditions. Typically, chicken, lamb, mutton (sheep), beef, or prawns are cooked in hot and spicy curry sauces. These are accompanied by rice, vegetables, and flat breads such as nan and chapatis. A main course is followed by milky desserts, such as bread cooked in milk and sugar or rice and milk. Sometimes a meal is finished with *paan*, which is a mixture of tobacco paste, spices, and betel nut spread on a betel leaf. The main drinks are a type of spiced milky tea known as chai; sugar cane juice; and *lassi*, a yogurt drink.

Celebratory dishes are served on festival days. A special dessert of vermicelli cooked in milk with almonds and pistachios is served on Eid ul-Fitr. The traditional dish at a wedding ceremony in Pakistan is chicken curry and rice.

? Did You Know?

Sharbat is a fruit drink made from squeezed fruits such as pomegranates, apples, melons, and mangoes. It is a Mughal drink and was the inspiration for modern-day sherbets.

▼ This shopkeeper in Rawalpindi is frying sweetened bread on a large iron griddle.

MUSIC

The most popular music of Pakistan is *Qawwali*, which dates back to the thirteenth century. Typically, *Qawwali* is made by a lead vocalist, two back-up vocalists, and a number of percussionists. The rhythm is traditionally played on a type of hand drum called a *dholak*. Poetic verses are usually mixed with a chorus and instrumental passages. Recently, some musicians have mixed *Qawwali* with Western pop music. This style has become popular with many young people in Pakistan. Among Pakistan's best-known musicians are Nusrat Fateh Ali Khan, the Sabri Brothers, and the Rizwan-Muazzam Qawwali Group.

▲ Pakistani brides at a ceremony in 2005. One woman wears a burqa, which completely covers her body, with just a slit for her eyes.

NATIONAL DRESS

The national dress of Pakistan is the *shalwar-kameez*, a combination of a long shirt over loose baggy trousers. Woman wear their *shalwar-kameez* in a variety of colors and designs, whereas men tend to stick to plain black or white. Muslim women are expected to wear conservative clothing such as the *shalwar-kameez* together with a veil or sometimes a burqa, which is a head-to-toe covering over the *shalwar-kameez*. Pathan men wear sleeveless embroidered vests (waistcoats) over their *shalwar-kameez*. Pakistani Pathans generally wear caps of various shapes, in contrast to Afghan Pathans, who wear turbans.

Focus on: Western Influences in Pakistan

Increasing globalization has strengthened the influence of Western culture in Pakistan, especially among the rich and the better-educated, who have easy access to Western goods, television, and food. Western-style clothing is commonly worn by the upper classes, and many Western food chains, such as McDonald's, have opened in Pakistan. Opposing Western influence, a reactionary movement within Pakistan wants to turn away from all Western influences and return to a more traditional Islamic way of life, with an emphasis on religion.

Focus on: Lollywood

Pakistan's film industry is often referred to as "Lollywood," because it is based in Lahore. Its films all tend to be similar—with love songs, dancing, fistfights, and good always defeating evil. During the 1960s, more than 200 films were made each year in Pakistan, and the stars of these movies were hugely popular in the country. Then, Pakistan's film industry went into a decline due to lack of investment. During the 1990s, barely 40 films were made a year. A revival took place in 2002 when Javed Sheikh, a well-known director, invested in digital equipment to make his hit movie *Yeh Dil Aap Ka Huwa (This Heart Belongs to You)*. Since 2002, a number of major digital films have been made in Pakistan, and the future of Lollywood is now looking brighter.

◄ Huge posters advertise the latest films being shown in Karachi movie theaters.

RELIGION

About 96 percent of Pakistanis are Muslims. The majority are Sunni Muslims, while the others are Shi'a Muslims. The remaining 4 percent of the population is made up of Christians, Hindus, and members of other faiths. These minorities are given fewer rights than Muslims. Non-Muslims, for example, may only vote for non-Muslim candidates. Violence between different religious groups has taken place in Pakistan over the years, particularly between Sunni Muslims and Shi'a Muslims.

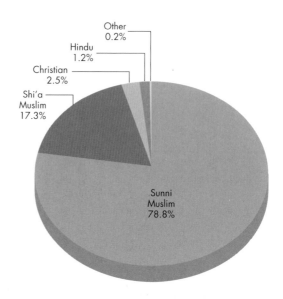

Other
0.2%

Hindu
1.2%

Christian
2.5%

Shi'a
Muslim
17.3%

Sunni
Muslim
78.8%

▶ Pakistan's major religions

FESTIVALS

Pakistanis celebrate a number of Muslim festivals, the most important being Eid ul-Fitr, Eid ul-Adha, and Eid Milad-un-Nabi. During these festivals, Pakistani people wear their best clothes to attend special prayers.

Eid ul-Fitr (often simply called "Eid") marks the end of the month of fasting known as Ramadan. In Pakistan, the night before Eid is called Chand Raat, or "night of the moon," and young women paint each other's hands with henna and wear colorful bangles. On the day of Eid, families attend prayers and then visit friends and relatives to eat a celebration meal and exchange gifts. It is a day of forgiveness, peace, fellowship, and unity. Eid ul-Adha celebrates Abraham's willingness to sacrifice his son to Allah. During the festival, Muslims sacrifice domestic animals, such as sheep or goats, and share the meat among their neighbors and relatives and with the poor. The festival of Eid Milad-un-Nabi celebrates the Prophet Muhammad's birthday.

The country also has a number of public national holidays, including Pakistan Day on March 23—the anniversary of the demand by the All-India Muslim League in Lahore in 1940 for a separate independent state for Muslims—and Independence Day on August14.

Focus on: Honor Killings

Each year hundreds of Pakistani women die in so-called "honor killings." These are women who are considered by the killers to have shamed their family. Among the many reasons given for honor killing are illicit sexual relationships, marriage without consent, rape, and seeking divorce.

Victims of honor killings are usually murdered by members of their own family, often in spite of the fact that their alleged crime is unproven. Although Pakistan has a law against honor killings, the murderers in these killings are rarely prosecuted, and the law is almost never enforced.

◀ A man in Karachi sells paper toys to celebrate the Muslim festival of Eid Milad-un-Nabi.

CHAPTER 12

Leisure and Tourism

The warm weather of southern Pakistan enables people to live an outdoor life. A favorite activity for young people living near the coast is to go to the beach. Favorite activities are very different in the mountains, where people tend to stay indoors during the long, cold winters and only participate in sports during the short summer months.

SPORTS

Many Pakistanis love sports. Pakistani men participate in many sports, especially cricket, hockey, squash, and tennis. Each year, Pakistan holds a National Games that covers a range of track-and-field events together with basketball, volleyball, cycling, weightlifting, and wrestling.

Pakistani teams also take part in the Olympics, the Asian Games, the Islamic Games, and the Commonwealth Games.

Many Pakistani people are passionate about cricket. It is the national sport, and most young boys play cricket. The national cricket team is admired, and its successes and failures on the field are reported in the newspapers and on radio and television. Pakistan's and India's cricket teams are great rivals. In 1992, Pakistan won the Cricket World Cup; the team's captain was Imran Khan.

Pakistan's men's field hockey team is one of the best in the world. The team has won gold

◄ Pakistan (in dark green) and India (in blue) are fierce competitors in field hockey. This match took place in India in 2004. Pakistan won 2-1.

◀ Polo is a fast-moving game played on horseback. This match is being played in the magnificent setting of the Shandur Pass in the Hindu Kush mountains.

medals at all the major field hockey events, including the Olympics, the World Cup, the Asian Games, and the Asian Cup. At the 2004 Athens Olympics, Pakistan did not win a medal, but the team's star player, Sohail Abbas, was the highest scoring player, with 11 goals.

Polo is incredibly popular in the country's mountainous regions. This is a sport in which two opposing teams of horsemen use sticks to move a ball around a field and score goals. Polo dates back to the sixth century B.C., when it was a training game for the cavalry. The game is played by two teams of six players, who play for two 25-minute periods with a ten-minute break. Pakistan's annual polo match played between teams from Chitral and Gilgit is fast becoming a major event on the tourist calendar.

A popular sport in South Asia is *kabbadi*. This sport is played by two teams of seven players. The teams take turns sending a raider into the opposing team's half of the field to tag members of that team and then return home. Any player who is tagged leaves the field. The raid must take place without the raider taking a breath. To prove this, the raider constantly chants. In Pakistan, the player chants "kabbadi."

Focus on: Women and Sports

In general, sports in Pakistan are for men and boys, while the women and girls concentrate on indoor activities such as needlework and cooking. In spite of the barriers, some young women in Pakistan do participate in sports. Most women in Pakistan do not play sports in public places to avoid being observed by men. Instead, they play on private playing fields and with only female spectators. They also wear baggy trousers and long-sleeved shirts to cover their legs and arms completely. A few female Pakistani athletes have competed in other Muslim countries. Pakistani women won a gold medal in golf at the 2005 Women's Islamic Games in Tehran, Iran.

► The Kalasha people live in three valleys near Chitral in the Hindu Kush. Kalasha women wear black gowns with elaborate, colorful decorations.

TOURISM

For a long time tourism in Pakistan has been underdeveloped. This lack of development is largely a result of the political unrest and wars in the region. Most visitors to the country are Pakistan-born people returning to see their families. The number of foreign tourists, however, is increasing, especially in the mountainous regions where trekking and mountaineering are growing in popularity.

The northern areas of Pakistan are very scenic and there are many old army fortresses, towers, and other architecturally interesting buildings with long histories. Some of the country's most beautiful valleys are found in the Chitral and Hunza Mountains in the Hindu Kush. Three isolated valleys near Chitral are famous for being the home of a small ethnic group known as the Kalasha people, who claim they are descended from soldiers in the army of Alexander the Great.

The Murree Hills and the Gallies are located about 34 miles (55 km) from Islamabad, at an altitude of 7,500 feet (2,286 m). They are the most popular summer resorts in Pakistan for wealthy Pakistanis and foreign tourists, as they have warm weather in contrast to the oppressively hot and humid weather on the plains. These resorts are equipped with modern facilities such as hotels, golf courses, chairlifts, and cable cars.

HISTORIC SITES

Punjab Province has a particularly rich history. Lahore, in Punjab, is usually regarded as Pakistan's cultural capital, and it attracts a large

Tourism in Pakistan

- ▭ Tourist arrivals, millions: 0.648
- ▭ Earnings from tourism in U.S.$: 763,000,000
- ▭ Tourism as % foreign earnings: 4.7%
- ▭ Tourist departures, millions: n/a
- ▭ Expenditure on tourism in U.S.$: 1,590,000,000

Source: World Bank

number of the country's tourists. The city was conquered by the Mughals, and its important monuments were built by them. For example, the Royal Fort, the Badshahi Mosque, Wazir Khan's Mosque, and the Tombs of Jehangir were built by the Mughals. In the south of Punjab Province, around Bahawalpur and Multan, many of the Muslim shrines, forts, and mosques feature the towers, courtyards, and domes, as well as the geometric shapes and bright colors, of much Islamic architecture.

Focus on: K2

K2, the second highest mountain in the world, is so named because it is the second peak of the Karakoram range. It was first conquered in 1954 by two Italians, Lino Lacedelli and Achille Compagnoni. Since that time, about 200 teams have successfully climbed the mountain. K2 is a technically difficult mountain to climb—harder than Everest, the world's highest mountain—and 50 climbers have died on the mountain. Most of these deaths occurred on the descent.

Among these buildings are the forts at Multan and Bahawalpur, the shrines of Sheikh Bahauddin Zakaria and Hazrat Shams Tabrizi at Multan, and the Tomb of Bib Jiwandi near Bahawalpur.

The ruins of ancient settlements have been excavated in the Indus Valley. They include the settlements of Moenjodaro and Harappa.

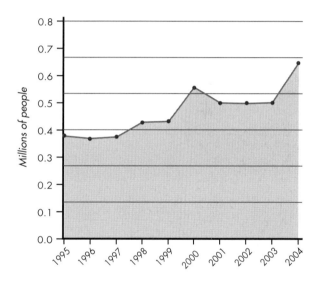

▲ Changes in international tourism, 1995–2004

◀ The tomb, or mausoleum, of the fourth Mughal emperor, Jehangir (1569–1627), lies about 3 miles (5 km) outside Lahore. It is built out of marble and red sandstone.

CHAPTER 13

Environment and Conservation

Pakistan suffers from a range of environmental problems, most of which are caused by its rapid increase in population, economic expansion, and the exploitation of its resources. In recent years, the government of Pakistan has focused on producing more food and energy to meet growing demand and on increasing economic growth. Controlling environmental pollution has not been a high priority. The effects of air pollution from traffic fumes and industrial emissions and water pollution from industrial wastes and sewage, however, are harming the health of the people.

AIR POLLUTION

In Karachi and Lahore, the level of air pollution is estimated to be 20 times higher than World Health Organization standards, and it is still rising. Islamabad is almost always shrouded in a thick layer of smog that hides the views of the surrounding hills. The major causes of Pakistan's air pollution are coal-fired power stations, traffic, and industrial emissions. The country's coal is of poor quality; when it is burned to generate electricity, it releases sulphur dioxide, a major cause of acid rain. Acid rain harms the health of trees, lakes, and rivers, and it also damages buildings. The areas of the country most affected by it are Karachi and the central Punjab.

Traffic fumes are another cause of air pollution in Pakistan. The average Pakistani vehicle emits as much as 25 times more carbon dioxide and 3.5 times more acid rain-forming chemicals than the average vehicle in the United States. The country has regulations to control vehicle emissions, but they are not strictly enforced. The main cause of this pollution is the use of poor-quality fuel that is high in lead and sulphur. Although unleaded gasoline is

► Although the burning of rubber has been banned, many factories in Pakistan, such as this brick kiln in Peshawar, continue to use rubber as a fuel. Burning rubber produces thick, black, polluting smoke.

available, most vehicles still run on leaded fuels, and few vehicles are fitted with catalytic converters. Motorized rickshaws are a particular problem in cities, because they use poor-quality fuels. The Canadian International Development Agency is working in some cities in Pakistan to convert rickshaws so they can run on LPG (liquefied petroleum gas), which is much cleaner.

DESERTIFICATION

Desertification is a problem in the arid regions of the country, especially in Baluchistan. This is caused by overgrazing of arid land by herds of sheep and goats. Once the cover of vegetation is lost, the soil is exposed and at risk of wind erosion. About 12 million acres (5 million hectares) are believed to be at risk of wind erosion. These problems can be solved by replanting and by better management of herds.

SALINIZATION

Poor water management in the irrigated areas of Punjab and Sind provinces is causing major environmental problems. Often, too much water is emptied onto the fields, where it causes waterlogging. In hot weather, water evaporates from the surface and leaves salts behind. This build-up of salt in the soil is called salinization. Soil that is damaged by salinization is too salty to grow most types of crops. In 1998, more than 14.8 million acres (6 million hectares) in Pakistan were thought to be unable to support crops because of salinization.

The problem of salinization can be overcome with better irrigation management and by growing varieties of crops that are more tolerant of high salt levels. In some cases, it is possible to wash salts out of fields by flooding them, although this uses a lot of valuable water.

▲ This farmer in Shimshal is altering the path of an irrigation channel. If irrigation is not carried out correctly, the soil can be damaged by waterlogging.

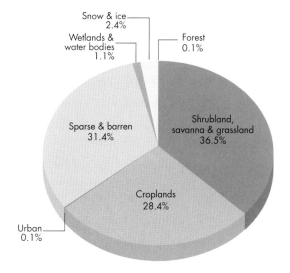

▲ Types of habitat

▲ Children in Karachi splash in filthy water. Every year in Pakistan, hundreds of thousands of children die from water-borne diseases.

WATER POLLUTION

Safe drinking water is essential for health, but millions of people in Pakistan do not have access to a source of safe water. All sorts of pollutants are emptied into Pakistan's rivers, lakes, and seas. They include untreated sewage, chemical wastes from factories, and pesticides and fertilizers from agriculture. Many industrial sites were built with little planning and with no wastewater treatment plants, so all forms of toxic chemicals end up in the country's water supply. As a consequence, about 40 percent of deaths in Pakistan are related to waterborne diseases. Much could be done to combat water pollution in Pakistan. Most important is to identify the industries that produce pollution and strictly enforce the National Environmental Quality Standards. This would require these industries to treat their wastewater to make it safe.

DEFORESTATION

Wood has long been an important energy source in Pakistan's rural areas. The rapid expansion of the country's population has led to an increased demand for firewood as well as for timber for building. Extensive deforestation, both of mangrove swamps along its coast and of forested slopes in the Himalayas, is a problem in Pakistan. The deforestation in the mountains has led to soil erosion on a large scale. The forested slopes protect the thin mountain soils, and the roots of the trees bind the soil. When the trees are felled, this protection is removed. Water flowing down the deforested slopes carries the soil with it. This can cause landslides and flooding.

In 1993, Pakistan's government prepared a Master Plan for Forestry Development that aimed to increase the country's forested area by 10 percent by 2018. Commercial plantations of fast-growing plants such as eucalyptus and bamboo have been planted in irrigated areas, and there has been some reforestation in the mountains. This program, however, has a small budget, restricting the amount of replanting and conservation that can be carried out.

NATIONAL PARKS

National parks in Pakistan were established in the 1970s to protect the country's forests and wildlife. Pakistan's first national park was Lal Suhanra (near Bahawalpur in Punjab Province) in 1972, followed in 1974 by Kirthar National Park (in southern Sind), which was set up to protect the ibex, the Chinkara gazelle, and the Urial sheep. The Khunjerab National Park, in the Hunza Mountains, was established in 1975. It is one of the country's most important regions for alpine biodiversity. At 16,405 feet (5,000 m), it is also one of the highest parks in the world. It protects the habitat of endangered species such as the Marco Polo sheep, the blue sheep, the snow leopard, and the snow cock (a type of bird). There are now 15 national parks in Pakistan, covering more than 1,764,000 acres (714,000 hectares). The country also has many wildlife sanctuaries and game reserves; one biosphere reserve, a protected area of high biodiversity; and two wetland sites that protect wildfowl such as swans and ducks.

Focus on: Oil vs. Wildlife

In 1997, great controversy erupted when Pakistan's government decided to allow oil and gas exploration in Kirthar National Park, which lies just north of Karachi. The park was established to protect rare and threatened species. Conservation groups, both within and outside Pakistan, tried to challenge this decision, because it violated Pakistan's international commitment to protect biodiversity. But the government simply changed the environmental laws, allowing the exploration to take place. The oil companies claim that development following the discovery of oil and gas in the park would have minimal impact on the environment and that it would provide local jobs.

Environmental and Conservation Data

- Forested area as % total land area: 0.1%
- Protected area as % total land area: 9.2%
- Number of protected areas: 205

SPECIES DIVERSITY

Category	Known species	Threatened species
Mammals	188	19
Breeding birds	237	17
Reptiles	189	9
Amphibians	17	n/a
Fish	137	3
Plants	4,950	2

Source: World Resources Institute

► The Khunjerab National Park lies high in the mountains of northern Pakistan. It was established to protect alpine species of plants and animals.

CHAPTER 14

Future Challenges

Pakistan is going to have to tackle a number of issues in the future, including its expanding population, environmental damage, the status of women, and the problem of Kashmir. There are also issues associated with economic growth and the threat of terrorism.

THE ROLE OF WOMEN

Although the status of women in Pakistan has improved in recent years, much is still to be done. Several groups, such as the Women's Action Forum, are tackling issues such as women's legal status, as well as everyday matters such as the dress code. Improved status for women may help to reduce the country's population growth, because educated women have a better understanding of health issues.

ECONOMIC FUTURE

There are a number of problems facing the stability of Pakistan's economy, including the country's foreign debt and its rising inflation. Pakistan's foreign debt is a great burden on the country, and it has a direct impact on the money available for social services such as education and health care. The government is tackling this problem by tightening financial controls in government departments so that less is wasted. In 2006, President Bush visited Pakistan and promised to try to secure a U.S.$3 billion aid package over five years. If successful, this would provide support to Pakistan's military in the struggle against terrorism and provide more resources for education and health.

KASHMIR – THE FUTURE

In January 2004, Pakistan and India started peace talks. India would like to formalize the current boundary between the two parts of Kashmir and make it an international border, an idea supported by the United States and Britain. Pakistan objects, claiming that this does not take into account the wishes of the Muslim population in Indian-controlled Kashmir. Pakistan's preferred outcome is for the whole of Kashmir to become part of Pakistan. However, although the majority of the population on the Indian side is Muslim, it also has a substantial numbers of Hindus and Buddhists who would object to joining Pakistan. An alternative is for Kashmir to become an independent state, but

◀ In April 2005, an important step toward peace took place when the first bus crossed from Pakistan-controlled Kashmir to India-controlled Kashmir.

◀ President Bush and President Musharraf respond to a question during a joint press conference in March 2006. President Bush visited Pakistan to strengthen the relationship between the United States and Pakistan.

this option is favored by neither Pakistan nor India, because both would have to give up territory and both countries fear that such a move would encourage other groups seeking independence. Currently the situation is a stalemate, with neither side wanting to change its position.

PAKISTAN AND TERRORISM

Pakistan has given support to the global fight against terrorists, and President Musharraf has clamped down on groups directly linked with al-Qaeda, even though these actions have not been popular with some of the radical Islamic groups in the country. In spite of these policies, Pakistan has continued to allow militant Kashmiris to operate in the country. Pakistan's government sees these militants as allies in its conflict with India, while India's government sees them as terrorists. In July 2006, seven bombs exploded on packed commuter trains in Mumbai (Bombay), India, killing more than 160 people and injuring hundreds. India's government blamed the militant Kashmiri groups, and stated that the peace talks could not continue until Pakistan's government cracked down on these terrorists. Pakistan needs to be seen to be fighting all terrorist groups, whatever their cause, if it is to win international support.

A BALANCING ACT

Pakistan has a difficult balancing act to perform over the next few years. The many ethnic groups within Pakistan have different demands. Some want more recognition while others want independence. China and the United States are underpinning Pakistan's economy with financial support; in return, both want more influence in the running of the country.

During 2005, the political situation in Afghanistan became more stable. There was a great increase in trade between Pakistan and Afghanistan. In 2006, however, the situation in Afghanistan changed for the worse. Hamid Karzai, Afghanistan's president, claimed that Pakistan was not doing enough to arrest members of al-Qaeda who were in Pakistan. The relationship between the two countries deteriorated, and President George W. Bush called the leaders to Washington, D.C., for talks. Relations between the two countries remain tense. Pakistan's relationship with India, however, is improving. India's economy is booming, and if Pakistan's government decides to cooperate more with India, it could share the benefits of its growing markets. Pakistan's future could be very prosperous.

Time Line

c. 4000 B.C. Indus Valley is a site of an early civilization.

c. 1700 B.C. Aryans from Central Asia move into the region.

327 B.C. Alexander the Great invades from the north and defeats the army of King Porus.

322 B.C. Reign of Chandragupta Maurya begins.

272–232 B.C. Reign of Ashoka.

195 B.C. King Demetrius of Bactria invades.

75 B.C. Scythians invade.

50 B.C. Parthians invade.

A.D. 120 Kushan dynasty established.

712 Imad-ud-din Muhammad bin Qasim invades Sind.

997–1030 Reign of Mahmud Ghaznavi and creation of Ghaznavid Empire.

1187 Muhammad of Ghor ends the Ghaznavid Empire.

1206–1526 Delhi Sultanate.

1526 Region becomes part of the Mughal Empire.

1615 British East India Company establishes base in India.

1700 Power of Mughal Empire begins to decline.

1857 War of Independence between British and Indians.

1858 Punjab and Sind along with India become part of the British Empire.

1907 All-India Muslim League established.

1940 All-India Muslim League demands a completely independent state of Indian Muslims.

1947 Partition of India. Pakistan becomes an independent country made up of East and West Pakistan. First Kashmir War with India.

1954 First ascent of K2.

1956 Pakistan becomes the Islamic Republic of Pakistan with a new constitution.

1958 Military take over and establish martial law.

1962 New constitution.

1965 Second Kashmir War with India.

1967 Islamabad becomes capital city of Pakistan.

1969 Martial law declared again.

1970 Awami League based in East Pakistan wins a majority in the Pakistani government, causing unrest across Pakistan.

1971 East Pakistan declares independence and forms the new state of Bangladesh. War with India and subsequent defeat. Zulfiqar Ali Bhutto elected as president.

1972 Establishment of first national park.

1973 New constitution.

1977 Zulfiqar Ali Bhutto overthrown in military coup. General Zia-ul-Haq imposes martial law and starts a program of Islamization.

1980s Millions of Afghan refugees flee to Pakistan.

1988 General Zia-ul-Haq dies in a plane crash, and Benazir Bhutto becomes the first woman to govern an Islamic country.

1990 Benazir Bhutto loses election, and Nawaz Sharif is elected prime minister.

1992 Pakistan wins Cricket World Cup.

1993 Benazir Bhutto wins election and becomes prime minister again.

1996 Benazir Bhutto's government dismissed on charge of corruption.

1997 Nawaz Sharif becomes prime minister.

1998 Pakistan becomes a declared nuclear power when it conducts tests of a nuclear bomb.

1999 Kargil Conflict in Kashmir. General Pervez Musharraf seizes power in a military coup. Nawaz Sharif found guilty of corruption and exiled to Saudi Arabia.

2001 Pakistan cuts contact with the Taliban in Afghanistan and joins United States and its "war on terrorism."

2002 U.S. reporter Daniel Pearl is kidnapped and murdered by Islamic extremists in Pakistan.

2003 President Musharraf survives two assassination attempts.

2004 A.Q. Khan, a Pakistani nuclear scientist, confesses to selling nuclear secrets; President Musharraf pardons him the next day. Shaukat Aziz becomes prime minister. Pakistan and India agree to a ceasefire in Kashmir.

2005 Cross-border bus service resumes in Kashmir. A powerful earthquake kills about 80,000 people and injures hundreds of thousands in northern Pakistan and Kashmir.

2006 President Bush visits Pakistan and promises to secure a U.S.$3 billion aid package over five years.

Glossary

acid rain rain that is more acidic than normal as a result of pollutants such as sulphur dioxide

Buddhism a religion based on the teachings of Siddhartha Gautama (c. 563–c. 483 B.C.), who became known as the Buddha, or "enlightened one"

catalytic converter a device that allows vehicles to run on unleaded fuel

constitution an basic set of rules and laws by which a nation, state, or other group is governed

corruption dishonest behavior

coup a sudden change of government, often by military force

deforestation the clearing of forestland, often by cutting and burning

delta the mouth of a river where the river spilts into many small tributaries

democracy a political system in which representatives are chosen by the people in free elections

desertification the process by which fertile land becomes desert as a result of the actions of people or climate change

erosion the wearing away of land or soil by the action of wind, water, or ice

ethnic having to do with the shared heritage, customs, beliefs, and, often, language of a group of people

federation a country that is made up of a number of self-governing states or regions

foreign debt the amount of money a country owes to overseas governments and organizations

foreign exchange the moving of money or currency from one country to another

fundamentalists people who hold strictly or literally to a religion or other set of beliefs

Gross Domestic Product (GDP) the total value of goods and services produced by a country

henna a type of dye from the henna plant that is often used to color skin or hair temporarily

Hinduism a native religion of India that worships many gods and goddesses and believe that a person is reborn many times into many different lives

hydroelectric power (HEP) electricity generated by harnessing the power of moving water

inflation the measurement of how much prices of a selection of goods that are necessary for life in a particular country change in one year

infrastructure the public facilities and services needed by a country to function, including roads, schools, hospitals, sewers, and water systems

irrigation the artificial watering of crops

Islam the religion based on belief in one God (Allah) and the teachings of the Prophet Muhammad

Islamization the practice of increasing emphasis on Islamic values and traditions

liquefied petroleum gas (LPG) a fuel made from a mixture of butane and propane that is stored in liquid form

martial law laws put in place when the military takes power in a country and civil laws are suspended

mass transit system a public transportation system designed to move large numbers of people

monsoon the seasonal winds that are generated by the difference in air temperatures over the Asian landmass and the sea that bring regular rainfall to the Indian subcontinent

mosque a Muslim place of worship

nomadic having a way of life that involves moving from place to place

partition to divide a single thing into more than one part; (capitalized) the name given to the division of British India into the separate nations of India and Pakistan

plateau high ground with a flat top

Qu'ran the holy book of Islam

rickshaw a small, two-wheeled cart for one passenger that is pulled by one person

salinization the accumulation of salts in the top layer of soil

sanctions a ban, usually on trading, used by nations to to compel another country to change its ways

Sharia Islamic law based on the Qu'ran

Shi'a having to do with Muslims who believe that religious authority can lie only with direct descendants of the Prophet Muhammad

silt fine particles of soil in rivers, ponds, or lakes

socialist a person who supports socialism, an economic system that favors the public ownership of major industries and distribution of wealth by the government

Sunni having to do with Muslims who believe that religious authority lies with the person best able to uphold the customs and traditions of Islam

Taliban a group of fundamentalist Muslims who seized power in Afghanistan in 1996 and ruled until 2001

temperate having a climate that is neither too hot nor too cold, with definite seasons

terrorists people who uses violence in order to scare others into giving in to their political demands

toxic poisonous, harmful

Further Information

BOOKS TO READ

Aykroyd, Clarissa. *Pakistan* (The Growth and Influence of Islam in the Nations of Asia and Central Asia). Mason Crest Publishers, 2005.

Crompton, Samuel Willard. *Pakistan* (Modern World Nations). Chelsea House, 2006.

Greenberger, Robert. *A Historical Atlas of Pakistan* (Historical Atlases of South Asia, Central Asia, and the Middle East), Rosen, 2003.

Haque, Jameel, and Katharine Brown. *Pakistan* (Countries of the World). Gareth Stevens, 2002.

Kovarik, Chiara Angela. *Interviews with Muslim Women of Pakistan*. Syren Book Company, 2005.

Kras, Sarah Louise. *Pervez Musharraf* (Major World Leaders). Chelsea House, 2003.

Padrino, Mercedes. *Benazir Bhutto* (Women in Politics). Chelsea House, 2004.

USEFUL WEB SITES

Ancient Indus Civilization
www.harappa.com/har/har0.html

CIA World Factbook: Pakistan
www.cia.gov/cia/publications/factbook/geos/pk.html

Indian and Pakistan: Fifty Years of Independence
www.cnn.com/WORLD/9708/India97/index.html

infopak.gov.pk: The Information Gateway to Pakistan
www.pak.gov.pk

Oxfam Cool Planet: Pakistan
www.oxfam.org.uk/coolplanet/kidsweb/world/pakistan/

UNICEF: Pakistan
www.unicef.org/infobycountry/pakistan.html

World Wildlife Fund: Pakistan
www.wwfpak.org

Publisher's note to educators and parents: Our editors have carefully reviewed these Web sites to ensure that they are suitable for children. Many Web sites change frequently, however, and we cannot guarantee that a site's future contents will continue to meet our high standards of quality and educational value. Be advised that children should be closely supervised whenever they access the Internet.

Index

Page numbers in **bold** indicate pictures.

acid rain 54
Afghanistan 4, 5, 9, 10, 15, 19, 21, 22, 25, 35–36, 59
agriculture 4, 6, 9, 15, 16, 29, 30, 55
air pollution **38**, 39, 45, 54–55, **54**
Alexander the Great 8-9, 52
All-India Muslim League 11, 49
al-Qaeda 36, 37, 59
Aryans 8
Ashoka 9
Awami League 12
Aziz, Shaukat 13, 23, **23**

Badshahi Mosque **10**, 53
Baglihar Dam 29
Baluchi people 18, 20
Baluchistan 5, 9, 10, 11, 15, 16, 20, 22, 25, 26, **26**, 27, 40, 55
Bangladesh 5, 12, **12**, 25, 37, 44
Bhutto, Benazir 13, **13**
Bhutto, Zulfiqar Ali 13, 25
Britain 4, 10–11
British India 4, 11
Buddhism/Buddhists 9, **9**, 58
Bush, George W. 36, 58, **59**

cellular phones 41, **41**
Chenab, River 16, 17, 29
China 4, 6, 9, 15, 30, 31, 35, 39, 40, 59
Christianity 6, 48
climate 16
clothes 47, **47**
coal 26–27, **27**, 54
Commonwealth of Nations 37
congestion 39
constitution 23
corruption 5, 12, 13, 21, 32
cotton 16, 30, **30**
cricket 50

dams 16, 28, **28**, 29
debt 33, 58
deforestation 56
Delhi Sultanate 10
desertification 55
deserts 15, **15**, 16

earthquakes 8, 17, **17**
East Pakistan 4, 5, 12, **12**
economy 6, 30–33, 58, 59
education 42–43, **42**, **43**
electricity 25, 26, 27, 28
emissions 39, 54–55
English 18

Faisalabad 21
Federally Administered Tribal Areas (FATA) 22
festivals **19**, 46, 49, **49**
floods 16
food 46, **46**

gas 25, 26, **26**, 57
Ghaznavid Empire 10
government 5, 22–25
Gwadar 40

Harappa 8, 53
health care 42, 44–45, **44**, **45**
Himalaya Mountains 4, 8, 14, 56
Hindu Kush 14, 52, **52**
Hinduism/Hindus 6, 8, 9, 10, 11, 13, 48, 58
hockey 50–51, **50**
honor killings 49
housing 20, 21
Hyderabad 19, 21, 31
hydroelectric power (HEP) 27, 28, 29

independence movements 25, 59
India 4, 5, 8, 9, 10, 11, **11**, 15, 19, 29, 31, 34, 44, 58, 59
Indian National Congress 11
Indus Valley civilization 4, 8, 53
Indus River 4, **4**, 8, 14, 15–17, 28, **28**, 29, 38
industry 21, 30–31, 35
Internet 41
Iran 4, 8, 31
irrigation 16–17, 28, 29, **29**, 55, **55**
Islam/Muslims 6, **6**, 10, 11, 13, 22, 23, 24, 25, 36, 37, 47, 48, 49
Islamabad 16, 20–21, 22, **22**, 39, 52, 54
Islamic Republic of Pakistan 12

Jhelum, River 16, 17, 28, 29
Jinnah, Mohammed Ali 11, 12

K2 14, **14**, 53
kabbadi 51
Kalasha people 52, **52**
Karachi **5**, 19, 20, 21, **21**, 31, **33**, **36**, 38, 39, 40, **40**, **48**, 54
Karakoram Highway 39, **39**
Karakoram mountains 14, **14**, 39, 53
Kargil Conflict 34
Kashmir 5, 13, 15, 17, **17**, 22, 28, 34, **34**, 39, 58–59, **58**

Lady Health Worker Program 45
Lahore **10**, **16**, **18**, 21, 31, 39, 40, **42**, **45**, 48, 52–53, 54
literacy 42, 44, 45
local government 24
Lollywood 48

madrassas **42**, 43
Mangla Dam 28
Mauryan Empire 9
military rule 5, 12–13, 22, 23
mineral reserves 15, 26
Moenjodaro 8, **8**, 53
Mohajir people 18, 19, 20
monsoon 16, **16**, 17
mountain passes 15
movies 48, **48**
Mughals/Mughal Empire 4, 10, **10**, 46, 53, **53**
Mujib, Sheikh 12
Multan 21, 53
Musharraf, Pervez 13, 19, 23, **23**, 24, 25, 36, 37, **37**, 59, **59**
music 47

Nanga Parbat 14
national parks 56–57, **57**
North West Frontier Province 5, 9, 11, 20, 21, 22, 24, 25
nuclear power 27, 35
nuclear weapons 34, 36

oil 25, 26, 31, 32, 57
Organization of the Islamic Conference, The (OIC) 37

Pakistan Muslim League 24–25
Pakistan People's Party 25
parliament 22–23, **22**
Partition 4, 11–12, **11**, 13
Pathan people 18–19, 22, 25, 35, 47
Peshawar **6**, 21, **24**, 40
political parties 24–25
pollution 6, 33, 39, 45, 54–56
polo 51, **51**
population 18–20, 54
ports 21, 40
Porus, King 8
poverty 6, 32, 33, **33**, 44
president 22–23
Punjab Province 5, 9, 10, 11, 15, 16, 17, 20, 21, 26, 30, 52, 55
Punjabi people 18

railways 35, 38, 39, 40, **40**
Rawalpindi 9, 20, 21, **46**
refugees 5, 19, 33, 35–36, **35**
religions 48

renewable energy 27, 28
rickshaws **38**, 55
roads 38–39, **38**, **39**

salinization 29, 55
schools 18, 42–43, **42**, **43**
Sharia law 24, 25
Sharif, Nawaz 13, 25
Sind Province 5, 10, 11, 15, 16, 19, 20, 21, 26, 28, 29, 55
Sindi people 18–19
soil erosion 33, 55
solar power 28
South Asian Association for Regional Cooperation 37
sports 50–51

Taliban 19, 36, 37
Tarbela Dam 28, **28**
telephones 41
television 40–41
terrorism 13, 36, **36**, 58, 59
textile industry 21, 30, 31
Thar Desert 14, 15, 16
tourism 52–53
transportation **5**, 38–40, **38**, **39**, **40**

United Nations 37
United States 6, 13, 30, 31, 32, 34, 36, 37, 54, 59
urbanization 20
Urdu 5, 18, 19, 43

war with India 5, 13, 34
water **15**, 16–17, 29, **29**, 45, 55, 56
water pollution 33, 45, 56, **56**
West Pakistan 4, 12
wind power 28
women 13, **13**, 23, 32–33, 43, **43**, 44–45, 47, **47**, 49, 51, 58

Zia-ul-Haq, General 13

About the Author

Sally Morgan is an experienced author of children's books and has written on a wide range of topics including nature and conservation, science, geography, and environmental issues.

She is particularly interested in wildlife and conservation and travels extensively to watch and photograph plants and animals.